If you've written off the church, I dare you to re

JOSHUA HARRIS, author of *Stop Dating the Church*

✳ ✳ ✳

Jesus loves the church. Yes, the church is imperfect, and we have made mistakes. But if we love Jesus, then we will love what Jesus loves. This book moves us to a thrilling portrait and future of what the church that Jesus loves and builds can look like and the hope we can bring to the world.

DAN KIMBALL, author of *They Like Jesus But Not the Church*

✳ ✳ ✳

Well, they've done it again. The *two guys* who *should be* emergent, but aren't, have followed up their first best seller with what I hope and pray will be a second. In *Why We Love the Church* DeYoung and Kluck have given us a penetrating critique of church-less Christianity and a theologically rigorous, thoroughly biblical, occasionally hilarious, but equally serious defense of the centrality of the church in God's redemptive purpose. In spite of her obvious flaws, DeYoung and Kluck really do love the church, because they love the Christ whose body it is. You don't have to agree with everything they say to appreciate and profit from this superbly written and carefully constructed book. This is a great read and I recommend it with unbridled enthusiasm.

SAM STORMS, senior pastor, Bridgway Church, Oklahoma City, Oklahoma

✳ ✳ ✳

If you're looking for reality, authenticity, and honesty, you've found it in this book. Kevin DeYoung and Ted Kluck, shrewd observers and faithful practitioners, have once again written a book that is like the best of foods—good tasting and good for you. Their style is easy, creative, and funny. They are theologically faithful, fresh, and insightful. They are sympathetic with many concerns and even objections to much in the church today, yet are finally defensive, in the best sense of the word. They are careful critics of the too-popular critics of the church. They are lovers of Christ and His church. I pray this book will help you love Christ's church better, too.

MARK DEVER, author of *9 Marks of a Healthy Church*

Two young men, a pastor and a layman, here critique the criticisms of the institutional church that are fashionable today. Bible-centered, God-centered, and demonstrably mature, they win the argument hands down. As I read, I wanted to stand up and cheer.

J. I. PACKER, professor of theology, Regent College

✳ ✳ ✳

If Jesus thought the church was worth dying for, it may just be worth living in. While not ignoring the sins of the church, DeYoung and Kluck remind us why church bashing is often shallow, and why the institutional church remains the most authentic place to encounter the good news of Jesus Christ.

MARK GALLI, senior managing editor, *Christianity Today*

✳ ✳ ✳

An attitude of indifference to the church has become tragically common within American Christianity. As a result, many people fail to make a solid commitment to congregational life and responsibility. The New Testament is clear—to love Christ is to love the church. Kevin and Ted provide a powerful word of correction, offering compelling arguments and a vision of church life that is not only convincing, but inspirational. This book will deepen your love of the church—and for Christ.

R. ALBERT MOHLER, President, The Southern Baptist Theological Seminary

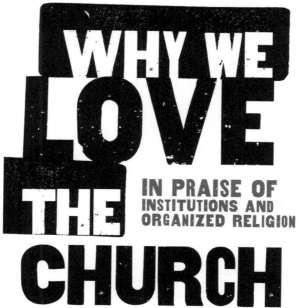

WHY WE LOVE THE CHURCH

IN PRAISE OF INSTITUTIONS AND ORGANIZED RELIGION

KEVIN DeYOUNG & TED KLUCK

MOODY PUBLISHERS
CHICAGO

Published in association with the literary agency of Wolgemuth & Associates, Inc.

Editor: Jim Vincent
Cover design and image: Studio Gearbox
Author photo: LCH Photography
Interior design: Smartt Guys design

Library of Congress Cataloging-in-Publication Data
DeYoung, Kevin.
 Why we love the church : in praise of institutions and organized
religon / Kevin DeYoung and Ted Kluck.
     p. cm.
Includes bibliographical references.
 ISBN 978-0-8024-5837-7
1. Church. 2. Apologetics. I. Kluck, Ted. II. Title.
BV600.3.D49 2009
262--dc22

2009010121

To University Reformed Church,
with love and gratitude

CONTENTS

The Church's one foundation

Is Jesus Christ her Lord;

She is His new creation

By water and the Word:

From heaven He came and sought her

To be His holy bride;

With His own blood He bought her,

And for her life He died.

"The Church's One Foundation,"[1] verse 1

OPEN BASEMENTS, BAD MARRIAGES, AND DECORPULATION

s a head still a head if it doesn't have a body? Is a basement still a basement if there's no house on top? Is a friend really your friend if you can't stand his wife?

According to 1 Corinthians 3, the church is God's building, with Jesus Christ as its foundation. To be sure, there can be no superstructure without a solid foundation. That's obvious. But it should also be obvious that no one lays a foundation unless he plans to build on it. No one drives past a cement foundation in the dirt and thinks, "Looks like they're about ready to move in." We know that a foundation exists to be built upon, not lived in all by itself. Who wants to live in a basement without the rest of the house on top? No one I know, except for the Christians who want Jesus but not the church.

More common than describing the church as God's building is the imagery of Christ and the church as husband and wife (Eph. 5:22–33; Rev. 19:6–9). Christ loves the church, gave Himself up for her, and makes her beautiful. The church submits to Christ, grows in beauty before Him, and obeys His commands. The two are one—now in preview, and later in fullness, but still they are one. They are inseparable as husband and wife. And any husband worth the paper his marriage license is printed on will be jealous to guard the good name of his wife. She may be a lying, no good, double-crossing poor excuse for a wife, but if she's your wife, you'll protect her honor, whatever may be left of it. And woe to the friend who comes around your house, hangs out, and expects to have a good time, all the while getting digs in on your bride. Who wants a friend who rolls his eyes and sighs every time your wife walks into the room?

Apparently, some people imagine Jesus wants friends like that. They roll their eyes and sigh over the church.

The Bible also tells us that the church is the body of Christ, with Jesus Himself at its head (Eph. 1:22–23). Every body needs a head to rule over it—to give it direction and purpose, to instruct it in the way it should go, to hold things together and give life to its members. Likewise, every head needs a body. I suppose in the world of science fiction heads could exist in vats or hooked up to a car battery or something. But in the real world, most of us don't see too many heads bobbing along apart from their bodies. If we ever did, I imagine our first instinct would not be to cuddle with the little cranium and sing it a love song. That would be a strange sight.

Strange though it may be, it is not unusual, at least not for some Christians. Increasingly, we hear glowing talk of a churchless Christianity. It is easy to read any number of personal memoirs where professing Christian men and women tell their tale of disenchantment with the local church and their bold step away from church into what, they would say, is a fuller, more satisfying Christian life. These days, spirituality is hot; religion is not. Community is hip, but the church is lame. Both inside the church and out, organized religion is seen as oppressive, irrelevant, and a waste of time. Outsiders like Jesus but not the church. Insiders have been told they can do just fine with God apart from the church.

DISMAYED AND DISMEMBERED

If *decapitation*, from the Latin word *caput*, means to cut off the head, then it stands to reason that *decorpulation*, from the Latin word *corpus*, should refer to cutting off the body. It's the perfect word to describe the content of this book. If our editors had been asleep at the wheel, we could have called it *Recent Trends in Decorpulation*. There is a growing movement among self-proclaimed evangelicals and in the broader culture to get spirituality without religion, to find a relationship without rules, and have God without the church. More and more, people are looking for a decorpulated Christianity.

Judging by the popularity of recent books like George Barna's *Revolution* and William P. Young's *The Shack* and the example of prominent Christians like John Eldredge, there are a lot of Christians who feel like current versions of church just don't cut it. More than a few have already left their churches, and the number of the disaffected seems to be growing. At the very least the "we want God, not an institution" mantra has struck a chord with many formal, informal, and former churchgoers. So we have books like *Life After Church, Divine Nobodies, Dear Church, Quitting Church,* and *So You Don't Want to Go to Church Anymore*, not to mention Frank Viola's church-as-we-know-it-is-all-wrong book *Pagan Christianity* and volumes like *UnChristian* and *They Like Jesus but Not the Church*, which explore why outsiders are turned off by the church.[2]

The narrative is becoming so commonplace, you could Mad Lib it:

The institutional church is so (pejorative adjective). When I go to church I feel completely (negative emotion). The leadership is totally (adjective you would use to describe Richard Nixon) and the people are (noun that starts with un-). The services are (adjective you might use to describe going to the dentist), the music is (adjective you would use to describe the singing on *Barney*), and the whole congregation is (choose among: "passive," "comatose," "hypocritical," or "Rush Limbaugh Republicans"). The whole thing makes me (medical term).

I had no choice but to leave the church. My relationship with (spiritual noun) is better than ever. Now I meet regularly with my (relational noun, pl.) and talk about (noun that could be the focus of a liberal arts degree) and Jesus. We really care for each other. Sometimes we even (choose among: "pray for each other," "feed the homeless together," or "share power tools"). This is church like it was meant to be. After all, (insert: "Where two or three are gathered, there I am in the midst of you," or "the letter kills, but the Spirit gives life," or "we don't have to *go* to church, we *are* the church"). I'm not saying everyone needs to do what I've done, but if you are tired of (compound phrase that begins with "institutional" or ends with "as-we-know-it"), I invite you to join the (noun with political overtones) and experience (spiritual noun) like you never will by sitting in a (choose among the following architectural put-downs: "wooden pew," "steepled graveyard," "stained-glassed mausoleum," or "glorified concert hall") week after week. When will the (biblical noun) starting being the (same biblical noun)?

This book is called *Why We Love the Church*, so you know where Ted and I are coming from. We don't want Christians to give up on the church. In fact, we hope that this book might have some small effect in helping people truly love their local church no matter how imperfect it may be and serve in it faithfully for the long haul. Perhaps, by God's grace, someone currently disenchanted with the church may decide to give it another chance after reading this book.

All that to say, this book is written for four kinds of people:

1. *The Committed.* Many reading this book are, no doubt, already faithfully attending and involved. We hope to spur you on to keep working hard and ministering steadily in your local church. Further, we hope this book can give you a thoughtful response to disillusioned former churchgoers you know and love.

2. *The Disgruntled.* Lots of churchgoers are still committed to the church but pretty ticked off at her limited impact and corporate failings. We sympathize with some of the frustration. But we also hope to show that the frustration is sometimes out of proportion to the offense and at other times misguided.

3. *The Waffling.* Here we are thinking of those who are currently in churches, but more or less uninvolved and quietly dissatisfied. To paraphrase the inimitable P. G. Wodehouse, you may not be disgruntled, but you are certainly far from gruntled. You are intrigued by the notion of churchless Christianity and wonder if checking out of Sunday morning might be the way to go. We hope to show you that such a move would be not only biblically unfaithful, but harmful for your soul.

4. *The Disconnected.* These are the ones getting the most press these days— the Christians (sometimes ex-Christians) who have left the church in their quest for God. Maybe you feel more spiritual than ever since leaving church or maybe you walked away years ago and deep down know you are

far from God. Or maybe, you are exploring a new kind of fellowship that seems way deeper and hipper than church ever was. In any case, we hope you will read this book with an open mind, considering what the Bible says about the importance of the church as organism *and* organization, as a community *and* an institution, as a living entity with relationships *and* rules. We hope, with you, to pay attention to the wisdom of that most neglected community—the community of the dead—and to listen for what the Holy Spirit may be saying through the Word of God to discern the thoughts and intentions of our hearts (Heb. 4:12).

WHY YOU/THEY/WE DON'T LOVE THE CHURCH

There are plenty of reasons people offer for their disillusionment with the church. These reasons can be grouped into four categories:

First, the missiological. Many Christians feel like the church just doesn't work anymore. They are just sick and tired of the church's failings and impotency. They recognize that most churches are not growing. "No one is getting baptized. Our young people aren't sticking with the church after high school. We have simply lost our way." Related to this concern, but somewhat distinct, many Christians criticize the church for losing sight of its mission. There are a host of problems in society that we are ignoring. The church has turned a blind eye to the community around her and is making no impact on the world. Face it, many people say, the church tried and failed. It's time for something completely different.

Second, the personal. Personal objections to the church are frequently voiced by both insiders and outsiders. The church, in the eyes of many outsiders, especially the young, is filled with hypocritical, antiwomen, antigay, judgmental, close-minded acolytes for the Republican Party. "Christianity," as one popular book puts it, "has an image problem."[3] And until we fix our image, the argument goes, more and more people will stay away from our churches and others will leave out of sheer embarrassment and frustration.

Many church insiders have an equally negative impression. They feel personally wounded or let down by the church. They find the church legalistic, oppressive, and hurtful. The leaders are controlling, the people are phony, and the ministry is programmed to death. The church is just another club, protecting its own and laying down a bunch of rules that only instill a sense of self-loathing and a fruitless desire to be good enough for God. Many in the church silently, or not so silently, feel like the Sunday services are a drag, the sermons are fluffy and uninspiring, and the music is prepackaged. The whole thing is, for some, a big, repetitive, soul-shriveling show. Who needs it?

Third, the historical. According to some disgruntled Christians, the church as we know it is an unbiblical, historical accident at best and a capitulation to paganism at worst. All that we think of as "church"—sermons, buildings, pastors, liturgy, offerings, choirs, and just about anything else you want to mention—are the result of the church falling from its pristine state in the first century into the syncretistic, over-institutionalized religion that now passes for Christianity. Whether this fall from grace came in the second century after the last apostle died, or in the first few centuries where Greek thinking overtook Hebraic thinking in the church, or in the fourth century with Constantine and all the accompanying evils of Christendom, the fact remains the same: the church as we know it in the West has been corrupted beyond recognition. And on top of this, we have the record of atrocities committed by the church over the centuries.

Surely history demonstrates that the church has, for the most part, been an embarrassing failure, the critics conclude. Let's say we're sorry and move on to some other way of building the kingdom.

Fourth, the theological. Most serious of all these important concerns are the biblical and theological critiques leveled against the church. Most Christians will acknowledge that "church" is an important New Testament concept and that Jesus loves the church and shed His blood for it. But for many, "church" is just plural for Christian. All you need for church is two or three people who worship Christ to be together in the same place. To be a part of a church means nothing more than that we love Jesus and love other people.

The organizational, institutional, hierarchical, programmatic, weekly services view of church, it is said, are completely foreign to the Bible. Jesus came to put an end to religion, not to start a new one. He came to bring the kingdom, not our little empires we call churches. The more we can move away from all the man-made doctrines, rituals, and structures of church as we know it, the closer we will be to truly knowing God in all His unconditional, untamed, mysterious, relational love.

TWO GUYS WHO LIKE GOING TO CHURCH (USUALLY)

As we did in our first book, *Why We're Not Emergent*, Ted and I have written completely separate chapters. Ted's chapters will be funnier, cooler, and more experiential. My chapters, well, they have many more endnotes. So it's a win-win situation. Come for the logic, stay for the laughs.

Actually, with Ted you'll get a wise, culturally savvy, yet orthodox, man-on-the-street, personal side of things. Read my chapters to get the historical, theological, and pastoral reasons why we love the church. My outline is simple. In my next four chapters I'll walk you through the four categories of disillusionment mentioned above. For each category, I'll try to explain the objection to the church, what we need to learn from it, and why we shouldn't swallow it hook, line, and sinker. I'll finish the book with an epilogue calling us to be a community of plodding visionaries.

In writing my chapters I hope to do more than just talk about people and ideas I disagree with. I really have no desire to make a career being the guy who finds errors in everyone else's thinking. I don't apologize for defending truth both positively and negatively—Paul and Jesus did the same all the time. But my aim is not to create an index of forbidden books and authors who are sick of church or don't go anymore. My aim is to present to the body of Christ, and for anyone else who cares to listen, a picture of why we should be in the church. Indeed, being part of a church—and learning to love it—is good for your soul, biblically responsible, and pleasing to God.

And I don't mean the "church" that consists of three guys drinking pumpkin spiced lattes at Starbucks talking about the spirituality of the Violent Femmes and why *Sex and the City* is really profound. I mean the local church that meets—wherever you want it to meet—but exults in the cross of Christ; sings songs to a holy and loving God; has church officers, good preaching, celebrates the sacraments, exercises discipline; and takes an offering. This is the church that combines freedom and form in corporate worship, has old people and young, artsy types and NASCAR junkies, seekers and stalwarts, and probably has bulletins and by-laws.

The church we love is as flawed and messed up as we are, but she's Christ's bride nonetheless. And I might as well have a basement without a house or a head without a body as despise the wife my Savior loves.

Kevin DeYoung

STYLES MAKE FIGHTS

When I want life wisdom, I often put aside books that are supposed to be full of life wisdom and listen to boxing trainers. Angelo Dundee, boxing trainer to Muhammad Ali and many others, said it best: "Styles make fights." And this, I guess, is a book about styles.

To further drag out the boxing metaphor, "organized" church—with its hierarchies, traditional leadership, and organizational structure—is taking a beating these days. It's Apollo Creed getting smacked around by the Russian in *Rocky IV*. People seem to want fellowship without commitment; they want to learn from each other, without being taught by anyone.

I was browsing a bookstore with my dad recently, whose reading tastes generally (always) fall into one of three categories: World War II aviation history, pro hockey, and the Bible. My dad is the most consistent Bible reader I've ever been around, which is only one of the reasons why I really admire him and value his opinion. And as we were walking down the religion aisle, looking at megadisplays for books like *The Shack* and *Everything Must Change*, he opined, rightly, that the greatest threat to the church will not come from outside the church, but from within. And while evangelicals are busy wringing their hands about Barack Obama, he added, we might be better served to wring our hands about this stuff.

These church books usually fit into one of two categories: the first being, "what I'm doing is awesome," and the second being, "what you're doing reeks." My hope and prayer for this book is that it fits into neither category. I've already written a "what you're doing stinks" book (*Why We're Not Emergent*) and I have no desire to do it again. And there are already way too many "what I'm doing is awesome" books out there. A lot of guys are patting themselves on the back for being revolutionaries, futurists, and trend shapers. There's nothing really wrong with that, but I just don't want to be one of them. In fact, what we're doing isn't revolutionary at all. It's awfully traditional and old. Feel the excitement.

And critiques of books like ours almost always (okay, always) include the terms "straw man" or "straw-man argument." Admittedly, I had to look up the term on Wikipedia for a refresher course shortly after the bullets started to fly when *Why We're Not Emergent* hit the shelves. For the record, Kevin and I have no desire or intention to set up men, straw or real, with the intention of then "knocking them down," which is the other phrase that appears often in these critiques. That said, the challenge of writing a book that will hopefully resonate with disgruntled former churchgoers as well as my dad, who likes church but dislikes most Christian books,[4] is a large one indeed.

MEET DISGRUNTLED JOHNNY

So rather than say "Disgruntled former churchgoer" each time we talked about this hypothetical burned-out, disaffected audience demographic, we named him (or her) Disgruntled Johnny. And when we talked audience, we often just substituted the name Disgruntled Johnny, which made it feel so much more personal. Maybe Disgruntled Johnny prays by himself in the woods each Sunday morning, having left the church several years ago. Maybe Disgruntled Johnny, encouraged by scores of articles, bumper stickers, and books, likes Jesus but not Christians (probably). He probably likes God but not "religion." There are a lot of Disgruntled Johnnies out there buying a lot of books in this vein. Without knowing it, Johnny has, suddenly, become a hot market.

And there are plenty of resources affirming Johnny in his disgruntled-ness. There are books telling him that it's okay to make his religion a "personal" thing. As long as Disgruntled Johnny downloads a sermon once in a while, or gets his "community" on a message board, or has a spiritual conversation at Starbucks he's okay. There's even a book now called *The Gospel According to Starbucks* by Leonard Sweet, where we can learn how to do church from the marketing kings of the coffee-and-suburban-hipster trade. And he (Johnny) is okay, in Jesus, but he's also missing out on all of the joys of organized, institutional religion, which now, culturally, is kind of like saying that there's a lot of joy inherent in getting a root canal procedure or doing your taxes.

To listen to the Disgruntled Johnny talk, you'd think evangelical church life is a big train wreck that is also leading people down the path of passion-less, uncreative, relationship-less destruction.

ABOUT LOVE AND INSTITUTIONS—
THEY CAN GO TOGETHER

Put simply, we're going to write a book about why we like (love) Christians. I know there are some obnoxious evangelical Christians out there. There are some at our church. I'm sure I am one at times. Christians also do weird, embarrassing things periodically (e.g., most Christian movies and a lot of contemporary Christian music). But there are also a lot of great people at our church—people whom I genuinely enjoy, and not just in a "he's my brother in Christ so I have to like him" sort of way. Some of them are even elders, or hold other "hierarchical" (this is a negative buzzword; note the tongue-in-cheek irony) positions within the church. And if my faith was strictly "personal," or if I just did house church with five other people, I would miss them dearly.

I'm also glad that my church is "organized." I'm glad I know where to put my toddler on Sunday morning. I'm glad somebody was institutional enough to think through topics for a Sunday school class or two. I'm glad my pastor, rather than just freewheeling it, cares enough to study Scripture and a bookshelf full of dead authors to give me real spiritual food each Sunday. I'm glad somebody leads a social outreach ministry to those less fortunate in our area. I'm glad somebody (not me) makes sure the kids are learning something biblical in their classes. It is, at its most basic, organized religion. And I love it.

But like Angelo Dundee so wisely pointed out, styles, even in church, make fights. We don't want to make fights. There's nothing about fights that makes me happy or holy in Jesus.

So while this book will be (hopefully) an encouragement to gospel-minded practitioners of organized religion both in the pew (me) and in the pulpit (Kevin), I also hope it will serve as an invitation to Disgruntled

Johnny to set aside his probably well-founded disgruntledness and join us in church. We're not perfect (far from it) but we love Jesus, we love the gospel, and we try our best to love other Christians.

Ted Kluck

NOTES

1. "The Church's One Foundation"; verse order from *Trinity Hymnal*, rev. ed (Suwanee, Ga.: Great Commission Publications 1990).
2. See Brian Sanders, *Life After Church* (Downers Grove, Ill.: InterVarsity, 2007); Jim Palmer, *Divine Nobodies* (Nashville: W Publishing, 2006); Sarah Cunningham, *Dear Church: Letters from a Disillusioned Generation* (Grand Rapids: Zondervan, 2006); Julia Duin, *Quitting Church* (Grand Rapids: Baker, 2008); Jake Colsen, *So You Don't Want to Go to Church Anymore* (Los Angeles: Windblown Media, 2006); Frank Viola and George Barna, *Pagan Christianity?* (Carol Stream, Ill.: Tyndale, 2008); David Kinnaman and Gabe Lyons, *UnChristian* (Grand Rapids: Baker, 2007); Dan Kimball, *They Like Jesus but Not the Church* (Grand Rapids: Zondervan, 2007).
3. Kinnaman and Lyons, *UnChristian*, 11.
4. He left the bookstore that day with a biography of hockey all-star Brett Hull and I left with a fantasy football magazine. Score one for secular publishing.

The Church shall never perish!

Her dear Lord to defend,

To guide, sustain and cherish,

Is with her to the end;

Though there be those that hate her,

And false sons in her pale,

Against both foe or traitor

She ever shall prevail.

—"The Church's One Foundation," verse 4

CHAPTER 1

THE MISSIOLOGICAL:

JESUS AMONG THE CHICKEN LITTLES

The word on the street is that the American church is gasping its last breath. To cite just one example, popular church consultant and conference speaker Reggie McNeal argues that while the situation in North America is not hopeless, things are worse than we think and the problems are more far gone than we imagined.[1] Unless the church in North America makes big changes (and fast), we are facing "sure death."[2] Even more strikingly, McNeal suggests that the new realities addressed in *The Present Future* "represent tectonic shifts in the ethos of the spiritual quest of humanity."[3] It doesn't get much more serious than that.

The church, according McNeal and many others, has lost its way, its influence, and its entire purpose. Without massive transformation, the church in North America will soon go the way of the dodo bird. In short, "the institutional church in North America is in deep trouble—and it should be, because it has lost its mission."[4] The church, then, has two choices: change or die.

McNeal is not the only voice crying in the wilderness. David Olson begins his helpful book, *The American Church in Crisis*, with this clear, if unsurprising, assessment: "The American church is in crisis."[5] Similarly, Neil Cole opines that "American Christianity is dying. Our future is in serious jeopardy. We are deathly ill and don't even know it."[6] "It's the institution of the church that's in its death throes," says another.[7] Not to be outdone, George Barna, who has grown increasingly disillusioned with what he has seen and measured among Christians in the last twenty-plus years, concludes very matter-of-factly based on his "research data" that "if the local church is the hope of the world, then the world has no hope."[8]

THE SKY IS FALLING (SORT OF, MAYBE)

Among those who feel like the church is almost or completely broken, two pieces of evidence are usually offered: (1) The church is losing people; and (2) the church has lost its mission. Let's start by looking at number one, the church's missing members.

The church in America, it is said, is dying a death of attrition. Our most faithful members, who also happen to be the most generous, are dying off. Young people are leaving the faith and not coming back. And the lost are harder to reach than ever. Ironically, as the mainstream media fears an impending Christian theocracy, Christians in America fear their own extinction, or at least their irrelevance.

Yet, the news is not all bad. In February 1939, pollster George Gallup started asking Americans "Did you happen to go to church last Sunday?" In that year 41 percent said yes. The wording has been altered slightly over the years, but basically the same question has been asked every year since. And the percentage responding "yes" has barely changed. From 2000 to 2005 the "yeses" in Gallup's church poll ranged from 40 to 44 percent.[9] In terms of actual attendance, we find that in 1990 on any given weekend 52 million people in America attended a church. In 2005, the number still stood at 52 million.[10] The wheels haven't fallen off yet.

But the news is not all good either. For starters, far fewer people actually go to church than the numbers suggest. It's called the "halo effect"—people give better answers to pollsters than they live out in real life. By one estimate, only 17.5 percent of the American public actually attend church on any given weekend, even though more than twice as many report that they do.[11] Furthermore, while the number of people in church has stayed the same over the past fifteen years (about 52 million), the percentage of churchgoers has decreased. Simply put, church growth has not kept pace with population growth. The same number of people may go to church, but since there are more people in the country, the number of churchgoers as a percentage of the whole goes down. So, according to Olson, while 20.4 percent of Americans went to church on any given weekend in 1990, only 17.5 percent went in 2005, and, by his estimates, only 14.7 percent will be in church on any given weekend by 2020.[12]

This is not a good trajectory. Anyone who loves Jesus Christ wants to see His church grow. But keep in mind that these numbers do not represent declining overall membership, but rather church membership that is not growing on pace with the increased population. This too is a problem. Believe me, I am not advocating an indifference to the lack of church growth in America. I want to see the percentage line going up, not down. And the fact that it is going down is worth our prayers and reflection (more on that shortly). But the claims of the church's imminent demise are grossly exaggerated. Even though only 17.5 percent of Americans attend on any given weekend (assuming this lower percentage is accurate), 37 percent still attend at least once a month, and 52 percent report belonging to some church tradition.[13] Again, I wish more people believed in Christ and that the people who claim church affiliation actually showed up in church every Sunday, but when over a hundred million people in this country attend church at least once a month, it seems a bit of a hyperbole to suggest that the church in America is about to disappear into thin air.

Moreover, when we look more closely at recent church decline we see that the decline has not happened uniformly across the board. Recall that from 1990 to 2005, the percentage of Americans in church on any given weekend fell from 20.4 percent to 17.5 percent. During the same time period the percentage of those attending the establishment mainline churches fell from 3.9 to 3.0 percent, while those attending a Roman Catholic church declined from 7.2 percent to 5.3 percent. But the percentage in evangelical churches was almost identical, going from 9.2 percent in 1990 to 9.1 percent in 2005.[14] Keep in mind these are percentages of the total population. This means the actual number of people attending an evangelical church on any weekend rose by several million over the last decade and a half. Almost all of the net loss in percentage of church attendance came from Catholic and more liberal Protestant churches. For example, in raw numbers, the mainline churches declined 21 percent in membership (from 29 million to 22 million) from 1960 to 2000, while at the same time overall church membership in the United States rose by 33 percent.[15]

So the story of declining church attendance percentage is not the story of a newfound dissatisfaction with the church at large, as much as it is the continuing story of Catholics and mainline Protestants losing their young (to evangelical churches or to no church), parents in mainline and Catholic pews not having as many children as evangelicals, and the old (who are found disproportionately among mainline churches) dying off.[16]

QUESTIONS FROM QUESTIONS

But for the sake of argument, let's look at the glass as half empty. Most of our churches are not growing. Even with all our megachurches, the evangelical community is not quite keeping up with population growth in the country at large. So how should we respond? Or to hit a little closer to home, how should *you* respond if your denomination or your church is shrinking, not only as a percentage of the whole but in real numbers?

Questions like these ought to prompt more questions. And the question the "disgruntled-with-church-as-we-know-it" books always seem to ask is the same: "What are we doing wrong?" In other words, the fix-the-church books almost always figure that declining church attendance, even as a percentage of the total population, means the church has messed something up. Even though the new crop of church books decry the old church-growth models, they still operate with the same basic assumption: namely, that churches should be growing and something is wrong with the church that isn't.

This assumption, however, is alien to the New Testament. Didn't Jesus say tell us that "the gate is narrow and the way is hard that leads to life, and those who find it are few" (Matt. 7:14)? Wasn't the early church of Philadelphia commended by the Lord Jesus even though they were facing opposition and had "little power" (Rev. 3:7–13)? There is simply no biblical teaching to indicate that church size is the measure of success. The renowned missiologist Lesslie Newbigin offers a wise summary:

> Reviewing, then, the teaching of the New Testament, one would
> have to say that, on the one hand, there is joy in the rapid growth

WHY WE LOVE THE CHURCH

of the church in the earliest days, but that, on the other, there is no evidence that the numerical growth of the church is a matter of primary concern. There is no shred of evidence in Paul's letters to suggest that he judged the churches by the measure of their success in rapid numerical growth, nor is there anything comparable to the strident cries of some contemporary evangelists that the salvation of the world depends upon the multiplication of believers. There is an incomparable sense of seriousness and urgency as the apostle contemplates the fact that he and all people "must appear before the judgment seat of Christ" and as he acknowledges the constraint of Jesus' love and the ministry of reconciliation that he has received (2 Cor. 5:10–21). But this nowhere appears as either an anxiety or an enthusiasm about the numerical growth of the church.[17]

In short, the church does not succeed or fail based on the ebb and flow of its membership rolls.

"ARE WE GETTING IN THE WAY OF THE GOSPEL?"

Having said that, I still think the question "What are we doing wrong?"—or to put it more theologically, "Are we getting in the way of the gospel?"—is a good one (for "successful" churches too I might add). As much as the verse as been abused, we don't want to ignore Paul's injunction that we be all things to all people in order that we might save some (1 Cor. 9:22). There are conservative churches who wear smallness as a badge of honor. Because they sense the real danger of measuring success by numerical growth, they think tiny churches are a sign of faithfulness and big churches are all sell-outs. Their pastors at times sound as though they're channeling John Owen, and their engagement with culture consists in explaining how modern-day Armenians differ from theological Arminians. They talk in the cadences of

32

another century and specialize in preaching to the choir. There are churches out there that not only don't grow, they are frankly proud that they don't. The church in America can shrink until it shrivels and dies as far as they are concerned. They are interested in truth not results.

There is much I admire about this attitude. It is refreshingly nonfaddish and unconcerned about worldly success. But those who hold this attitude are often blind to the ways in which they make it unnecessarily hard for people to feel at home in their churches. They can be inflexible about the wrong things and unable to see how the unbeliever is not always entirely to blame for disliking the church. So, "Are we getting in the way of the gospel?" is a worthwhile question to ask.

OTHER QUESTIONS WORTH ASKING

It's just not the only question worth asking. That's my complaint with so many of the "church is lame" books, both those from the church growth vein and those from the emergent/missional approach. They assume that every decline in attendance, every negative perception of the church, every unsolved societal problem, and every unbeliever still wandering outside our doors, is an indictment on the "way we do church." If people aren't coming to know the Lord in droves and our communities aren't transformed into a multicultural city on a hill, then there must be something dreadfully wrong with church as we know it. "Surely, it's time to change. If not everything, then most everything," they argue.

But there are other questions we need to ask when we don't see the results we desire. Questions like:

• *Are we believing the gospel?* People won't be convinced of Christianity if they don't sense we are convinced of it. This is especially true when doubt and disbelief come from the pulpit. As Richard Baxter (1615–91) noted in his own day, some of our churches are pastored by unregenerate men. Even more have preachers who are either confused about the gospel or simply cold to it. Just a century later (in 1740), George Whitefield concluded that "the generality of preachers [in New England] talk of an unknown and unfelt Christ. The reason why congregations have been so dead is because they have had dead men preach to them."[18]

• *Are we relying on the power of the gospel?* If the gospel is "the power of God for salvation to everyone who believes" (Rom. 1:16), why don't our services and our evangelism focus more explicitly on the good news of Christ's death and resurrection for the forgiveness of sins? Likewise, if our churches are shrinking, perhaps it is because the role of the Word has shrunk in our preaching and witness. Do we really trust God to build His church through His Word, or do we rely on tricks and gimmicks?

• *Are we getting the gospel out?* It sounds simple to some, and hopelessly fundamentalist to others, but if we want to see the church grow, we need to actually get out and tell people about the good news of Jesus. Church growth will not keep pace with population growth unless we actively share the gospel with nonChristians and winsomely plead with them to be reconciled to God.

• *Are we getting the gospel right?* In an age where many Christians assume that doctrinal precision gets in the way of mission, we would do well to remember that Paul damned to hell anyone, including himself, who messed with the content of the gospel (Gal. 1:8). God blesses churches that remain faithful to His Word. "We will repeatedly suggest," write sociologists Roger Finke and Rodney Stark in beginning their survey of the churching of America from 1776–2005, "that as denominations have modernized their doctrines and embraced temporal values, they have gone into decline."[19] When it comes to doctrinal boundaries and moral demands, the history of the church in this country demonstrates that stricter is stronger.[20] We cannot expect the church to grow when she proclaims a false gospel.

• ***Are we adorning the gospel with good works?*** We must watch closely our doctrine and our life (1 Tim. 4:16). As we'll see in the coming chapters, people will not listen to our message or be attracted to our churches if they see hypocritical Christians and churches unconcerned about the problems of the world. Our good works are not the gospel, but they can adorn it and make it more attractive (Titus 2:10).

• ***Are we praying for the work of the gospel?*** We must pray for more workers, pray for soft hearts, pray for God's Spirit to supernaturally bring about new birth. If we truly believed in God's sovereignty, discouraging trends and statistics would cause us first to pray. Every bit of hopelessness is a reminder to hope in God and an impetus to prayer.

• ***Are we training up our children in the gospel?*** A good portion of the decline in church attendance comes from the failure to retain our own children. What will it profit a man if he transforms the world but loses his own children? We should also consider that church growth is covenantal as well as evangelistic. If we want the church in America to grow, we should consider how God might be calling some of us (but not all) to grow our own families.

THE QUESTION OF A SOVEREIGN GOD

To all these questions, I could add one more: "Are we trusting God's sovereignty in the gospel?" God causes the deaf to hear and the blind to see. He melts hearts of stone and hardens others. Paul did not always see a favorable response to the gospel. Neither will we. God may send a season of blessing and revival or He may use us, like so many of the prophets, to give one last warning of the judgment to come. Some will plant, some will water, and some will reap a harvest.

Our part is to do our part. Church decline or stagnation can lead us to evaluate ourselves in all of the above categories. But only God saves. It is right to plan and pray for "results" and plead with others to know Christ, but no one can change the number of God's elect.

OUR PART IS TO DO OUR PART. BUT ONLY GOD SAVES.

Remember that on that "great gettin' up morning," God will not reward churchgoers, or His churches for that matter, for being big and influential, or hip and culturally with-it, but for being good and faithful (Matt. 25:23). That's all God asks of us—be good and faithful, which is right, because that's the best we can do.

THE MISSION OF GOD

The second piece of evidence that critics offer of the church's alleged failure is its lack of purpose and mission. Missional churches are "in" these days. Social action is hot. Evangelism is regarded as too aggressive (just a sales pitch), modern (cold, logical argumentation), and condescending ("my God is better than yours"). Service and justice ought to be the church's chief concerns. As one author has said, "Your job is to bless people; that's the covenant. Don't have an evangelism strategy—have a blessing strategy."[21] A generation raised on seeker-sensitive churches where all the energy and value seemed to be on getting the unchurched into our worship services has reacted against an all-or-nothing commitment to getting people saved. So gone are the days where churches put all their focus on unchurched Harry and Mary. Now the emphasis is on human trafficking, AIDS, poverty, the homeless, and the environment. To bring Christ's kingdom of peace, justice, and blessing to the world is the mission of God (*missio dei*) for the church.

And, according to many young and emerging voices, the church is largely failing in this mission. We've "abdicated our role [as messengers of hope] and covered up our lights. We stand by and watch as people struggle with poverty, depression, and dysfunction. We see people oppressed and killed around the world, and do little or nothing."[22] The church should be starting schools that provide a just education for minorities, establishing homeless shelters, setting up mentoring and adoption programs, developing programs that place the elderly into homes of younger families, and making the problems of the Third World our first priority.[23] According to one church-leaver, the church has done so little to help local communities that the neighborhoods can't help but be "very disappointed" in the church and "embarrassed to be a part of you."[24] In short, we've been putting all our efforts into institutional survival when our goal should be community transformation.[25]

He Who Has Ears Let Him Hear

Before I offer a critique of this missional critique, let's recognize that one's background can color how a person will value the missional position. If you have been a part of a church or denomination that has held up evangelism as the only noble Christian calling, then a broader missional perspective is going to be welcome. If your church was suspicious of any kind of social ministry—relief, development, medical, education, you name it—then going "missional" probably sounds freeing. If you have been a part of an angry, backbiting, constantly splitting, culturally insulated church, then an emergent church or no church at all starts to sound pretty attractive. By contrast, if you have been around more liberal mainline Christians, like I have in my denomination, or around reformed Christians lacking in evangelistic passion, like I have and sometimes have been, then the missional literature starts to sound suspect, like recycled social gospel or another moralistic endeavor that overlooks the eternal plight of the lost.

I realize I hear the missional critique of the church with certain ears. I haven't been a part of a church that makes "secular" work second rate. I've never attended a seeker church that made saving the lost the only legitimate ministry. I've never been a member of a hard-nosed fundamentalist church that considered social ministry a waste of time because "it's all going to burn up anyway." I've seen plenty of church cheesiness in my day, but I've never been to a church that offered spiritual milk fit for baby Christians every week. My antennae are more attuned to other imbalances.

All that to say I want to take from the missional folks what is good: a passionate concern for social problems, a zeal for helping the least of these, and a call to go out into the world instead of trying to make the church look like the world so they will come to us. These are just a few of the themes I appreciate in the missional approach to and critique of the church. But I also have several concerns.

Changing the World

For starters, the purpose of the church in missional circles is often reduced to one thing: community or global transformation. This point is repeated several times, but it is never really defended. All Christians agree that the gospel has social implications. Most probably agree that community transformation could be a good thing. But where do we see Paul talking to his churches about transforming their communities? Where does Jesus, with the corrupt oppressive Roman Empire in full sway, seem interested in world-changing initiatives? It may be implied in passages about the cosmic lordship of Christ or living good lives among the pagans or praying for the king, but the concerns of the New Testament seem to have little to do with explicit community transformation.

Moreover, the missional notion of community transformation is quite narrow. As one author says, "Instead of raising awareness of the evils of some fictional book, why not work toward raising literacy in your community's schools? Instead of forming groups to oppose gay marriage, why not work with an AIDS clinic or involve yourself in seeking justice for this oppressed group."[26] Leaving aside whether homosexuals are oppressed or not, why is working at an AIDS clinic kingdom work but opposing gay marriage is not? If the kingdom is where God reigns and His rule is honored and His way of life lived out, then there are no unrepentant homosexuals in the kingdom (1 Cor. 6:9).

The two groups that talk most about bringing the kingdom are dominionist/theonomist types and the emergent/missional crowd. Dominionists think, "All of creation belongs to Christ. It must all submit to His kingly rule." So they want to change laws and influence politics and exercise Christ's dominion over the world. On the other end, missional types think, "Jesus came to bring the kingdom of God's peace and justice. We must work for shalom and eliminate suffering in the world." Fascinating—one group goes right wing, seeking to change institutions and public morality, and the other goes left wing, wanting to provide more social services and champion the arts.

Both camps have a point, but both are selective in their view of the kingdom, and both have too much "already" and not enough "not yet" in their eschatology. We need to remember that when the disciples asked Jesus before His ascension whether He was now going to restore the kingdom, He not only told them no, but He told them their main responsibility was to be

His witnesses (Acts 1:6–8). We are less the reincarnation of Christ in the world ushering in His kingdom and more His ambassadors bearing testimony to His life and finished work (2 Cor. 5:20).

The Church in the World

We also need to reflect more carefully on the difference between the responsibility of the church's calling and the individual Christian's calling. Without this distinction, the church gets overwhelmed and overburdened with good ideas. For example, I've read books that suggest that the church ought to: participate in food distribution; help people find employment; offer parenting classes; help inner-city residents with issues of poverty, drug abuse, and education; adopt a city in the developing world; start an adoption program; and place the elderly in families. The church also should partner with the YMCA; begin classes for literacy and math; help people with car repairs and financial help; sponsor family movies; and organize soccer and baseball leagues. According to the missional crowd and many of those frustrated with church as we know it, this is the sort of kingdom work the church needs to be about.

Indeed, all these ideas are fine. I like them, and I hope my church might be able to do a few of them. But when these activities are the main responsibilities of the church as church, we run into a couple of problems.

First, we will be forever failing as the church. The church will look abysmal when we are expected to be the cure-all for a large portion of our societal problems. In her book on leaving the church, Sarah Cunningham tells about surveying the citizens of her own Michigan town for their impressions of the church and how the church could do more in the community. One lady responded by saying:

We've already got tons of churches. Look around. There's a church on every corner. I bet you could count nine or ten within three blocks of here. . . . And nothing has changed, has it? . . . People don't have enough job training or employment opportunities. Drunks wander the streets. The same homeless people have been circling in and out of the shelters for the last fifteen years. Kids don't have anything to do to keep them out of trouble. Meanwhile, the churches keep right on existing, holding their services every Sunday. And it never changes anything. It seems pretty obvious to me that churches are not the answer."[27]

At this point the author expresses her disappointment and embarrassment with the church. But does the continuing presence of problems in our communities really demonstrate the failure of the church? It could, I suppose. Maybe all the churches in her Michigan town care zippo about everyone and everything outside their doors. But some things probably are better off because there are churches on every corner. I imagine some problems are not as bad as they could be because of Christian programs and witness in that community. Do we assume police officers are worthless because we still have crime or parents are pointless because kids still do stupid things? Not at all. Why then do we assume that the existence of an unmet need or ongoing tragedy in the world is unassailable proof of the church's failure?

I am certainly not advocating carefree indifference. Apathy may be all some churches are currently offering in the way of "help." But my hunch is most are doing better than that—not as good as they could be, but not as bad as many think. Besides caring for the people in their own congregations—and Galatians 6:10 commands us to "do good to everyone, and *especially* to those who are of the household of faith" (emphasis added)—many churches help those outside her walls. Most churches I know support at least some missionaries who work with disaster relief or economic and agricultural development in the two-thirds world. Most churches send out work trips to paint, build, or reconstruct houses. Most churches probably support a local food pantry or deliver meals on wheels. Many churches are involved in rescue missions or AIDS relief overseas or teaching English to internationals or visiting the elderly in nursing homes. Other churches have jail ministries and adoption programs, and open their buildings to the community. Still others send shoe boxes full of toys overseas, support hospitals, or do after-school tutoring.

This may not be enough—it never will be—but each of these actions is something, and a good deal something more than nothing. Before we castigate ourselves for caring so little about social justice, let's not miss all the significant work going on right under our noses. Dull church budgets, pimply mission trips, traditional Christmas offerings, and a hundred other programs our churches do year after boring year all help people near and far.

The Christian in the Community

Besides all this, we have the work that individual Christians do. Isn't that the work of the church too? To be sure, more can and should be done, but many Christians are already involved in salt-and-light activities—as they run their business according to Christian principles, serve the less fortunate through Community Mental Health, bring their faith to bear in movies and television, and disciple young people as public schoolteachers. It simply boggles my mind when I read George Barna conclude based on his research that "local churches have virtually no influence in our culture . . . The local church appears among entities that have little or no influence on society."[28]

Come on, really? What research shows that? Are we actually to believe that if every church were removed from every street corner in America and every Christian in those churches disappeared that the impact on our culture would be negligible? Are a hundred million Christians really that pathetic?

In my community, Christians staff the rescue mission and churches host soup kitchens. The Christians around here take collections for food pantries, personal needs banks, and furniture giveaways. Individual churches offer cribs, car seats, teddy bears, books, budget counseling, pots and pans, diapers, coats, and clothes, while other churches contribute to these collections and a Christian organization coordinates all the moving parts. There are hospice programs for the dying, centers for the aging, and agencies to help with adoption, foster care, and refugee assistance—all run by Christians.

Of course, Christians in mid-Michigan aren't the only ones doing good things and Christians aren't doing all the good things we could. We are better at giving to people and programs at a distance than actually entering into relationships with dirty, messy lives. But we don't have to pretend we are starting at zero. In almost any town, in any part of the country, you can find churches and Christians "being the church" in a thousand different ways that make an enormous difference in their communities.

Second, if the main work of the church as church is in the social services realm of community involvement, aren't we forgetting what makes us unique? If global change or community transformation is our main goal, we may get some good stuff done, but then we'll become political—as happened in the church on the left in the 1960s and 1970s, on the right in the 1980s and 1990s, swinging back to the left in the 2000s—and we'll become redundant. There's nothing uniquely Christian about caring for the poor or distributing micro-loans. That's not to say we can't do them with Christian motivation or even that we can only do things if no one else does them. But, as Richard John Neuhaus has said, the first political task of the church is to be the church.

Please understand. Community engagement *is* good. It's all too easy to criticize the missional crowd without actually doing anything yourself. And yet, a critique is warranted. The vision behind words like "missional" and "kingdom" often ends up reducing the church to a doer of good, noncontroversial deeds (e.g., no mention of pro-life concerns as important to community transformation) like every other humanitarian organization. When young people talk about the church getting involved in social justice, they almost always have in mind sex trafficking, oppression and death in Darfur, AIDS, or some other social cause. The danger for conservative evangelicals is to dismiss these concerns as liberal issues that don't concern us. I really don't want that to happen. I can feel it in my own heart sometimes—"Sex trafficking is a trendy emergent issue; I don't want anything to do with it." This is a sinful response.

But there are dangers for the social justice crowd too. Most of their causes demand nothing of us Christians except psychological guilt and advocacy. This often means that middle-class kids feel bad about being middle class and complain that other people (the church, the White House, multinational corporations, those fat cats on Wall Street, etc.) aren't doing more to address these problems. The problems are almost always far away and the solutions involve other people caring more.

There's also the danger that we only champion issues that win us cool points. Let's be honest, no one we run into is for genocide or for sex trafficking or for malnutrition. It takes no courage to speak out against these things. We can be thankful that in these areas the world's values (in our world at least) overlap with Christian virtues. But where is the outrage from missional folks about abortion, casinos, the threats to religious free speech, and other evils that plague our world? We all have different callings. Some may be drawn to pro-life issues and others to addressing global hunger, but let's make sure as Christians that our missional concerns go farther than those shared by Brangelina and the United Way.

What makes the church unique is its commitment, above all else, to knowing and making known Christ and Him crucified. True, the biblical story line is creation, fall, redemption, *and* re-creation. But the overwhelming majority of Scripture is about our redemption, how God saves lawbreakers, how sin can be atoned for, how rebels can be made right with God. We haven't told the story of the Bible if we only talk about what God will do with the cosmos and we avoid mentioning the blessing or curse that will fall on individuals depending on their response to Jesus. It seems to me that proclaiming this message of redemption is the main mission of the church, even more than partnering with God to change the world through humanitarian relief and global activism.

Recently, Dan Kimball, who literally wrote the book on the emerging church, offered his honest assessment of the success of the "missional" church. I quote Kimball at length because his comments are refreshingly candid and provide a needed balance to the anti-megachurch, antipreaching, antiprogram rhetoric that passes for sophisticated analysis in our day.

> We all agree with the theory of being a community of God that defines and organizes itself around the purpose of being an agent of God's mission in the world. But the missional conversation often goes a step further by dismissing the "attractional" model of church as ineffective. Some say that creating better programs, preaching, and worship services so people "come to us" isn't going to cut it anymore. But here's my dilemma—I see no evidence to verify this claim.
>
> Not long ago I was on a panel with other church leaders in a large city. One missional advocate in the group stated that younger people

in the city will not be drawn to larger, attractional churches dominated by preaching and music. What this leader failed to recognize, however, was that young people were coming to an architecturally cool megachurch in the city—in droves. Its worship services drew thousands with pop/rock music and solid preaching. The church estimates half the young people were not Christians before attending.

Conversely, some from our staff recently visited a self-described missional church. It was 35 people. That alone is not a problem. But the church had been missional for ten years, and it hadn't grown, multiplied, or planted any other churches in a city of several million people. That sure seems to be a problem if the church is claiming to be "missional."

Another outspoken advocate of the house church model sees it as more missional and congruent with the early church. But his church has the same problem. After fifteen years it hasn't multiplied. It's a wonderful community that serves the homeless, but there's no evidence of non-Christians beginning to follow Jesus. In the same city several megachurches are seeing conversions and disciples matured.

I realize missional evangelism takes a long time, and these churches are often working in difficult soil. We can't expect growth overnight.

I just wish that the missional church would be slow to criticize "attractional" churches that are making a measurable impact. By impact, I don't mean just numbers. I am not enamored by how many come forward at an altar call. In fact, I am a bit skeptical of how numbers are generally counted and used. I am also not defending my own church here. I am not part of a megachurch, but am part of a four-year-old missional church plant. But I am passionate about Jesus-centered disciples being made. And surprisingly, I find in many large, attractional churches, they are.

Something not helpful in all this discussion is even calling structured churches "attractional." Yes, these churches have music, preaching, or children's programs that can be considered "attractive," but there is more to these structured or large churches than simply the programming. When you study these churches and hear the actual stories of people who have trusted in Jesus, you find that the *attraction* for the unchurched was not the programs or music. It was the Spirit of God in the lives of the Christians who are part of these churches. They were the ones who represented Jesus in such a way that the non-Christians became "attracted" to what God is doing in their lives. . . . We can never forget the urgency of being on mission to those who do not know Jesus yet.

There are so many who don't understand the joy of Kingdom living here on earth and the future joy of eternal life. This joy motivates me missionally, but I also cannot forget the horrors of hell. This creates a sense of urgency in me that pushes me past missional theory to see what God is actually doing in churches—large and small, attractional and missional. . . .

Where are new disciples before being made? Where are healthy disciples being grown? I hope and pray that we won't criticize other forms of church who are seeing new disciples being made.

I would rather be part of a Christ-centered church of any size full of "attractional" programs where people are coming to know Jesus as Savior than part of a church that uses "missional" language but people are not coming to know Jesus as Savior.[29]

After finishing *Why We're Not Emergent*, I exchanged several e-mails with Dan Kimball. I have no doubt that we still disagree on some important issues and approaches to ministry, but he impressed me as a solid evangelical who wants to see people saved from hell, believe in Jesus, and be a part of the church. Kimball believes in the indispensability of evangelism, and this counts for a lot.

John Stott, with typical evenhandedness, explains that mission "includes evangelism and social responsibility, since both are authentic expressions of

IT IS BIBLICALLY AND ETERNALLY NECESSARY THAT WE VERBALLY TELL PEOPLE THE GOSPEL.

the love which longs to serve man in his need. Yet I think we should agree with the statement of the Lausanne Covenant that 'in the church's mission of sacrificial service evangelism is primary.'"[30] This means that our "blessing strategy" in mission must involve proclamation—the actual using of words to communicate the gospel so that by putting their faith in Christ, the covenant blessing of Abraham might come to all who believe (Gal. 3:14). We don't want to fall for the old "deeds not creeds" slogan or the confused aphorism, "preach the gospel and use words only when necessary." No matter what the trendmeisters recommend, it is absolutely biblically and eternally necessary that we verbally tell people the gospel and call people to faith and repentance in Jesus Christ.

THE LOST GOSPEL

What's missing from most of the talk about the kingdom is any doctrine of conversion or regeneration. The kingdom of God is not primarily a new order of society. That was what the Jews in Jesus' day thought. They did not understand that you must be born again to enter the kingdom of God (John 3:3, 5) and without holiness no one will inherit the kingdom of God (1 Cor. 6:9–10). Faith and repentance, and the godly life that follows in their wake, are unchangeable requirements for membership in the kingdom. We aren't just out to refurbish some morals or intervene in global crises. We want to live like Christ, show people Christ, and make a difference for Christ, but also call people to renounce their rebellion against God, flee worldliness, and be ready to meet the King when He returns to finally establish His kingdom.

We need to be careful about our language. I think I know what people mean when they talk about redeeming the culture or partnering with God in His redemption of the world, but we should really pick another word. Redemption has already been accomplished on the cross. We are not co-redeemers of anything. We are called to serve, bear witness, proclaim, love, do good to everyone, and adorn the gospel with good deeds, but we are not partners in God's work of redemption.

Similarly, there is no language in Scripture about Christians building the kingdom. The New Testament, in talking about the kingdom, uses verbs like *enter, seek, announce, see, receive, look, come into*, and *inherit*. Do a word search and see for yourself. We are *given* the kingdom and *brought into* the kingdom. We testify about it, pray for it to come, and by faith it belongs to us. But in the New Testament, we are never the ones who bring the kingdom. We receive it, enter it, and are given it as a gift. It is our inheritance. It's no coincidence that "entering" and "inheriting" are two of the common verbs associated with the Promised Land in the Old Testament (see Deut. 4:1; 6:18; 16:20).[32] The kingdom grows to be sure, and no doubt God causes it to grow by employing means (like Christians), but we are never told to create, expand, or usher in the kingdom just as the Israelites were not commanded to establish Canaan. Pray for the kingdom, yes; but not build it.

Most importantly, I have a hard time hearing the gospel in the missional critique of the church. At best, the gospel is about a "relationship with Jesus."[32] At worst it is nothing but a "personal life-transforming experience"[33] and "people realizing their full potential as beings created in the image of God."[34] It's possible to put a good face on all these euphemisms, but this is not a clear gospel.

When I hear people getting sick of church, I almost always see at the same time a minimizing of, or growing indifference toward, or ambiguous terminology for such phrases as "substitutionary atonement," "justification by faith alone," "the necessity of faith and repentance," "the utter inability of man to save himself," and "the centrality of the cross and resurrection." I really want to assume that the new missional Christians still believe we are

> **JESUS' DESCRIPTION OF THE CHURCH FOCUSED NOT ON CHANGING THE WORLD BUT ON THE HOPE OF ETERNAL LIFE.**

sinners in need of grace, and that Jesus' death paid our debt and propitiated the wrath of God, and that we must repent of our sin and trust in Jesus alone for our salvation. I want to assume this, but I wish I didn't have to. I wish the glory of Christ crucified, the offense of the cross, and the necessity of conversion were more explicitly stated and more clearly central.

I can't help but feel that lurking beneath the surface in much of the current disillusionment with the church is a dis-ease with the traditional message of salvation (see chapter 3). People are passionate about the poor, the environment, and third-world debt. But they seem embarrassed by a violent, bloody atonement for sin, let alone any mention of the afterlife that hangs in the balance. Everyone, it seems, has a vision for the church that Jesus talked about in Matthew 16:18—the church against which the gates of hell shall not prevail. Many people read this today as a word about the church's role in liberating the oppressed, bringing shalom, or storming "the authority structures and control centers of evil."[35] But the reference to the "gates of hades" is a Jewish euphemism for death (see Isa. 38:10, which uses the Hebrew term *sheol*). Jesus' initial description of the church focused not on changing the world but on the hope of eternal life.

My observation is that as people grow tired of hearing about the atonement, salvation, the cross, and the afterlife, they grow tired of church. Because the more that sin and redemption and heaven and hell recede into the background, the more the church becomes just one among several options for making a difference in the world.

So as much as the church has been nothing but a holy huddle at times and as much as I admire zeal for good works, there is a danger in much of the missional literature that the gospel of God's grace toward sinners gets swallowed up in urgent calls for world redemption and cultural transformation. There is a danger of centering our churches on adopting schools and offering parenting classes instead of being centered on the message of a heavenly Father who adopts unworthy children of wrath through the work of His Son on the cross. There is a danger that we find our unity in doing good missional deeds for our community and not in the good news of the gospel. There's a danger our Christianity becomes all imperative and no indicative, all about what we need to do with God and little about what God's done for us. There's a danger that when people get disinterested in the gospel, they get disinterested in the church. And once they leave the church, they've left the only institution whose mission aims for eternity and whose gospel is truly good news.

NOTES

1. As quoted in David Kinnaman and Gabe Lyons, *UnChristian* (Grand Rapids: Baker, 2007), 145.
2. Ibid., 119.
3. Ibid., xviii.
4. Ibid., 141.
5. David T. Olson, *The American Church in Crisis* (Grand Rapids: Zondervan, 2008), 15.
6. Neil Cole, *Organic Church* (San Francisco: Jossey-Bass, 2005), 91. Later in this same paragraph, Cole says "This is the mentality in Christian 'churchianity.'" But I think the "mentality," which is clearly an unhelpful one for Cole, refers to the desire "to keep current organizations alive for as long as possible" not to the sentiment that American Christianity is dying. On page 33, he says the church "is deluded into thinking she is well, when indeed she is deathly ill."
7. Quoted in Tony Jones, *The New Christians: Dispatches from the Emergent Frontier* (San Francisco: Jossey-Bass, 2008), 137.
8. George Barna, *Revolution: Finding Vibrant Faith Beyond the Walls of the Sanctuary* (Carol Stream, Ill.: Tyndale, 2005), 36.
9. Olson, *Church in Crisis*, 26. Barna's polling numbers for the same question ranged from 43 to 47 percent for the same time period.
10. Olson, *Church in Crisis*, 28, 34–35.
11. Ibid., 28.
12. Ibid., 180. Likewise, each year church planting (4,000 per annum) continues to outstrip church closures (3,700 per annum), so that the total number of churches in America is increasing (by 300 per annum). The growth is not keeping up with increases in total population, which Olson estimates necessitates a net of over 3,000 new churches a year (147).
13 Ibid., 28–31.
14. Ibid., 36.
15. Michael S. Hamilton and Jennifer McKinney, "Turning the Mainline Around: New Sociological Studies Show That Evangelicals May Well Succeed at Renewing Wayward Protestantism," *Christianity Today*, August 1, 2003, at http://ctlibrary.com/16902, as cited in Olson, *Church in Crisis*, 146–47.
16. See Joseph Bottum, "The Death of Protestant America," *First Things*, August/September 2008, 23–33.
17. Lesslie Newbigin, *The Open Secret: An Introduction to the Theology of Mission,* rev. ed. (1975; repr., Grand Rapids: Eerdmans,1998), 126.
18. Quoted in Roger Finke and Rodney Stark, *The Churching of America 1776–2005* (New Brunswick, N.J.: Rutgers Univ. Press, 2005), 53.
19. Ibid., 9.

20. Ibid., 249.

21. Reggie McNeal said this at a live One Thing conference in 2008; see http://www.rca. org/Page.aspx?pid=3721. See also Brian McLaren, *Generous Orthodoxy* (Grand Rapids: Zondervan, 2004), 120–23.

22. Steve Conrad, "I'm Sorry: One Christian Apologizes to the World" in Spencer Burke, *Out of the Ooze* (Colorado Springs, NavPress, 2007), 22.

23. Brian Sanders, *Life After Church* (Downers Grove, Ill., InterVarsity, 2007), 116–17.

24. Sarah Cunningham, *Dear Church: Letters from a Disillusioned Generation* (Grand Rapids: Zondervan, 2006), 21.

25. Reggie McNeal, *Present Future* (San Francisco: Jossey-Bass, 2003), 26.

26. Mike Derschon, "Counter-Consumer Culture," in Burke, *Out of the Ooze*, 95.

27. Cunningham, *Dear Church*, 20–21.

28. Barna, *Revolution*, 118.

29. "Dan Kimball's Missional Misgivings" found at *Leadership Journal*, Fall 2008, http://blog. christianitytoday.com/ outofur/archives/2008/12/dan_kimballs_mi.html. The text has been modified to reflect Kimball's original submission to *Leadership Journal* (with minor corrections from Kimball himself).

30. John Stott, *Christian Mission in the Modern World* (Downers Grove, Ill.: InterVarsity, 1975), 35.

31. See Brian Vickers, "The Kingdom of God in Paul's Gospel," *The Southern Baptist Journal of Theology*, 12, no. 1 (Spring 2008): 62.

32. McNeal, *Present Future*, 82.

33. Ibid., 17.

34. Ibid., 73.

35. Brian McLaren, *Everything Must Change* (Nashville: Thomas Nelson, 2007), 118. See also Cole, *Organic Church*, 10; and Cunningham, *Dear Church*, 166.

Every revolutionary ends up either by becoming

an oppressor or a heretic.

 — Albert Camus

We have a lot of people revolutionizing the world

because they've never had to present a working model.

 — Charles F. Kettering

CHAPTER 2

GETTING OFF THE ROAD AND GETTING BACK TO CHURCH

I could be wrong, but I fail to see how two privileged CEOs stroking the perfect nine-iron shot on a Sunday morning constitutes revolutionary behavior. In his revolutionary book entitled, appropriately, *Revolution*, George Barna seems bent on convincing us that two yuppies who are "bored" and "burned out on a church that wasn't using their considerable intellect and talent" are, in fact, committing a par-four revolutionary act.

He goes on to explain that these two men no longer had time for Sunday morning worship in their busy schedules, so in true type-A CEO-ish fashion they multitasked by taking their quasi-spiritual conversations to the links on Sunday morning. David (the good one) points out the grandeur of the mountains that God made. Michael (the nonrevolutionary backslider) just wants to banter playfully about golf. The take-home value is that there is a big revolution afoot, and we Christians, like David (the golfer, not the king of Israel) had better be a part of it.

BEING REVOLUTIONARY

Barna seems intent on branding this revolution as the Next Big Thing in evangelical life, and reminds us of how good he is at predicting Next Big Things, as evidenced by his 1990 book *The Frog in the Kettle*. There are lots of "will you be on board?" types of statements that seem to suggest that if you're not a revolutionary, you and your church may very well be left in the spiritual dust. Let me preface this whole thing by admitting that this is the first Barna book I've ever read, and I came into the experience with a certain amount of awe for George Barna simply because I had often heard or read the words: "Barna research shows that . . ."

Perhaps my expectations were too high. Or perhaps I'm just sick of revolutionaries. I am thirty-two years old, and am a part of the generation that has probably purchased more Che Guevara posters than any other generation in history. You know the poster. It's the one that shows Che bearded, in his beret, looking larger than life. It is often accompanied on the wall by a Bob Marley poster, or the John Belushi poster in which he wears a sweatshirt emblazoned with the word "College." We're big on revolutionaries. We're big on changing the world. We're big, also, on not being ordinary.

A search on a popular Christian bookseller's Web site revealed no less than sixty-two items with the word *manifesto* in the title and hundreds containing the term *revolutionary*. There are revolutionary books for teens. Ditto for stay-at-home moms. There's a book about how Jesus was a revolutionary communicator, and how you can use His revolutionary communication skills in your home/business/church. The question then becomes, If we're all revolutionaries, are any of us an actual revolutionary? Being a revolutionary used to mean that you overthrew a government; now it means that you're a courageous enough visionary to have church on a golf course or in someone's living room.

My point in all of this is not to make not-so-subtle jabs at revolutionary culture (maybe a little bit); rather, it is to encourage the scores of nonrevolutionaries in our midst, of which I am one. I want to encourage those of us who try really hard to pray for our families and friends, try to read our Bibles consistently, and share the gospel with those around us. Those of us who aren't ready to chuck centuries worth of church history, and years of unglamorous but God-glorifying growth in the name of revolution.

ON MEMOIRS AND ON-THE-ROAD STORIES

I'm also a part of the generation that has produced more memoirs before the age of thirty-five than any other in history. We're crazy about Christian narrative nonfiction, especially those "on the road" stories, no matter how trite or contrived they may be. We're journeyers. We're wanderers. We still haven't found what we're looking for. Jack Kerouac's (or Donald Miller's…or Lauren Winner's) wayward children are all over the Christian book landscape.

These narrative titles all follow a similar pattern, in that in them experiences are had (a cross-country road trip, a self-finding excursion through Europe, a documentary chronicling the lameness of American Christians, a chronicle on how the author dropped out of church and subsequently "found" Jesus), and then those experiences are shared in book form. Many of these books are supposed to tell us that "community" is the answer, and individualism is bad, but at the end of the day these books are largely about the individual and his or her discoveries.

Sometimes these discoveries are good, edifying, and helpful. Sometimes they're just bizarre, as in Sarah Cunningham's *Dear Church: Letters from a Disillusioned Generation* in which she writes about the edifying impact of an Eminem concert, due largely to all the diversity she finds in the audience. With all due respect to Eminem[1] and Sarah Cunningham, sometimes I think we've all lost our minds.

We seem to look to the profane first in an attempt to co-opt its coolness as our own, and then to attempt to draw out nuggets of edification from it.[2] When *The Sopranos* was one of the highest rated cable TV shows, author Chris Seay wrote "*The Sopranos* has the power to lead you to greatness as it amplifies the wretchedness in us all."[3] With all due respect to Chris Seay and James Gandolfini, I'm all too aware of my own wretchedness, and watching Tony spout a string of profanities and whack people in increasingly interesting ways[4] doesn't exactly leave me feeling like I'm on a road to greatness or sanctification.

With that rather large disclaimer, my chapters are also in this narrative vein, and I will also, at times, try to co-opt someone else's coolness as my own. But it's all done with a noble goal in mind, and that is to get you to think about liking church again. To try to convince you that in the midst of the constant, low-level drone of conversation about community, culture, "missional," and "finding God," there is a place to worship, sing praises to our King, live in community, and grow in sanctification. And it's church.

In *Lord, Save Us from Your Followers*, Dan Merchant takes the popular "A Christian making fun of Christians" tack, and uses it to engage the world in conversations about how Christians just aren't getting it done. He plasters himself in bumper stickers (Jesus Fish, Darwin Fish, Pro Life, Pro Choice, etc.), and he raps with liberal funnyman Al Franken—and when I say "funnyman" I do actually mean that Franken is funny, although when most conservative writers say "funnyman" they mean it derisively, in a way that suggests that not only is this person not funny, this is a person I just don't like. In Merchant's book and documentary, he seeks to answer the question: Why is the gospel of love dividing America?

My question is, Why wouldn't the gospel of love divide America? It divided Israel. It divided families (Lot and his wife). It ruined friendships (David and Saul) and it even pitted man against himself on occasion (Peter, denying Christ three times before the cock crowed, feeling hor-

> **WHY WOULDN'T THE GOSPEL OF LOVE DIVIDE AMERICA? THE GOSPEL IS, BY NATURE, OFFENSIVE.**

rible about it, but then ultimately experiencing Christ's forgiveness). What Merchant fails to realize is that the gospel is, by nature, offensive. It suggests that we are in fact sinners in need of salvation. Jesus tells His disciples that they will leave behind friends, careers, and even family members for the sake of the cross. He is, essentially, suggesting that if the gospel isn't divisive in some way it's probably no gospel at all.

Merchant channels Donald Miller in another "Confession Booth" chapter, in which Merchant, like Miller, mans a confession booth at a Gay Pride event to apologize for the ills perpetrated by Christians. The promotional material promises that this will be both "controversial and moving." I understand the spirit in which these apologies were written (I think). But I think it's awfully easy to apologize for something that was done almost a thousand years ago (see: the Crusades) by someone who isn't you. In essence, these authors are saying, "I'm really sorry for the things that people who aren't nearly as cool, forgiving, or enlightened as me have done."[5] I know that Christians have done all manner of horrible things, but I also think humility is only half the story.

* * *

DISGRUNTLED TEDDY

As we talked about this manuscript with the publisher, the publisher some-times had helpful ideas like "make it authentic." Now, "authentic" means different things to different people. For some, it may be your carefully dish-eveled hair, lovingly agonized-over faux-retro Johnny Cash T-shirts, and tattoos. For others, it's woundedness. For still others, (and perhaps most), it's a marketing thing. Authenticity, in Christendom, is now a big seller.

When publishers say "be authentic," what they really mean is, "Share some of your own struggles with the church." They want me to describe my "phase." That is, they want me to talk, in the past tense, about the time that I felt church was lame, how I got through it, and how I got to where I am now, which is, ostensibly, loving church and growing. The loving-church-and-growing part is basically true, most of the time.

I let this simmer for a few weeks, confident that, as a pro, I can accu-rately reconstruct my most disgruntled time with the church in a way that will be helpful and instructive for all of the Disgruntled Johnnies reading out there in American Church Land. Unfortunately, I run into one snag: I think I might be in my church-is-hard phase now.

ONE SUNDAY MORNING

It's 8:57 on a Sunday morning in May and I'm running late for church. The service starts at 9:15 and it's imperative that we show up on time because we're waving a crazy looking flag for a kids' thing we do at our church called "children in worship." The flag amounts to a bamboo stick with a couple of ribbons tied around it, and the idea is that you walk up front, hoisting the flag in the air, and the kids follow you out of the service, up the aisle, and then upstairs to a classroom where you basically have Sunday school[6] with them.

We haven't had breakfast yet, so we swing into a Tim Horton's, where I insist on eating inside even though we're late. In the roughly twelve minutes we're inside, I drop my wife's yogurt parfait onto the floor, we have an argument (not about that, about something else), and my five-year-old decides he no longer likes sprinkles on his doughnut, and instead wants to eat mine. (He does.) The coffee, though, is perfect.[7]

As I speed down I-496 on the way to the Trowbridge Road exit, I think through all the reasons that I don't want to be going to church. I'm tired. I spent the majority of the week on the road, speaking at a Christian conference where I, honestly, took a nice, long vacation from my problems.[8] At times, conference speakers can think of themselves as real sacrificial road warriors, out there surviving travel-related issues all for the sake of "The Kingdom." But sometimes—this morning for me—we are reality-averse wussies who just want to leave their parenting problems, marital challenges, and church frustrations behind so that we can have people say encouraging and flattering things about our book or speech.

Please . . . No Church Today!

Here are all the reasons—numbered, but in no particular order—why I don't want to go to church this morning and am in a bad mood:

1. *Everybody in our church is pregnant.* My wife and I have been trying to conceive a child now for several years. Unfortunately, our church is located in mid-Michigan's fertile crescent—it seems that every woman between the ages of nineteen and forty-three is getting pregnant and having a baby every eleven months. Every female conversation seems to involve any combination of the following: length of labor, how far along they are, breast-feeding, or whether they "went"[9] early. To say the least, this has been devastating for my wife, who I think, under the circumstances, has

been a real trouper for simply getting out of bed and walking through the lobby every Sunday. So far we've only walked out of one infant baptism.

For the record, we're happy for all of these people, and many of them are among our best friends on earth. Today, my wife is doing very well in this regard, but I'm the one with the attitude. One time I found out via phone that one of our friends had a new baby girl and gave her the name that I wanted to name the baby girl that we'll probably never have. For some reason this news hit me like a nine iron to the crotch and I've stayed depressed about it for a few days now.

2. *It feels like everybody in our church, except us, homeschools.* In addition to feeling like you have to have at least six kids to be a real family, it also sometimes feels like the only spiritual thing to do is homeschool those kids. This never felt like a good fit for us, and while we've had wonderfully honest conversations with our dear friends about this, where they've affirmed us in our choices[10] and we've done the same for them, it's still weird for Tristan (and us) that he's the only public-schooler in the lot. Other students do their home-school field trips, study their home-school textbooks, and play in their home-school soccer leagues all together, without us. It feels like we're always battling the perception that they're handing out condoms and guns at the doorway leading to Tristan's public-school kindergarten class—which has only happened once or twice (kidding).

3. *Meet and greet.* "Turn to those in the row behind you and greet them this morning, while we play some piano music." I have hated, and always will hate, meet and greet for the obvious reason that it feels really inauthentic and awkward. But that said, I understand why churches try to do it.

4. *Sometimes we sing worship songs in different languages* like Spanish, Korean, and Shona. This shouldn't bother me, but it does this morning for some reason, though it feels good to admit in print that the problem

is entirely with me. Someone in our church once asked me if I thought it made Spanish-speakers in our body feel welcomed when we sing "Santo, Santo, Santo" ("Holy, Holy, Holy"), to which I replied, "I hope so," which was to imply that it doesn't do anything for me. I'm a horrible person.[11]

5. *Sometimes we don't know who our friends are.* See items 1 and 2 above, re: homeschooling and everybody being pregnant. When many of your friendships are dependent on these "stage of life" similarities, it can sometimes feel discouraging when those stages of life seem to divide people.

Far from Perfect

As it turns out, church is rarely as bad as I sometimes think it's going to be, though for the record we do sing "Santo, Santo, Santo" this morning and during the congregational prayer the pray-er spends several minutes thanking God for all of the "new babies and pregnant women" in the congregation. I squeeze my wife's hand. If she smiles and rolls her eyes with me I'll know she's okay with it. If not, it could be a long day.

CHURCHES HAVE COOL PEOPLE. CHURCHES HAVE DORKS.

Still, I probably dislike going to church more now than in the past because the above reasons hold pretty true on so many Sundays.

Our church is far from perfect. The parking lot is too small. Sometimes I don't like the music. And, often, I feel like an outsider, but not for the usual reasons that "leave your church and find God" authors give for feeling like outsiders, which usually include, but are not limited to, tattoos, piercings, liberal politics, and conservative politics.

This in-and-out dynamic is nothing new, in churches or in pretty much any other aspect of society, as is illustrated by high school. Churches have cool people. Churches have dorks. Churches have the popular rich kid, the prom queen, the jock (as men's basketball nights and softball leagues have painfully illustrated), the drama kids (as churches experimenting with Sunday morning skits have also, painfully, illustrated), and the rebels.

* * *

THE GOSPEL ACCORDING TO HUGE, MULTINATIONAL CORPORATIONS

Here's to the crazy ones. The misfits. The rebels. The troublemakers. The round pegs in the square holes. The ones who see things differently. They're not fond of rules. And they have no respect for the status quo.

You can praise them, disagree with them, quote them, disbelieve them, glorify or vilify them. About the only thing you can't do is ignore them.

—From an Apple Computers ad in 1997

Submission to authority isn't going to sell anyone a computer. We love to think of ourselves as misfits, rebels, and troublemakers, and then use that vibe to create something so fantastic that we're able to throw all of our outsiderness back into the face of those who made us feel like outsiders. This has worked brilliantly for Apple, the computer company that might be the most effectively marketed business on the planet. What they've done is create a corporate structure and product line that really works from a bottom-line, cash flow perspective, and then they've convinced each user that they're getting in on the ground floor of something very exciting and rebellious—even though there seem to be almost as many Mac users as PC users these days.

The idea is that if you buy a Mac, you'll be the slender guy in the coffee shop arranging all of his video clips into a short film with music that takes the Telluride Film Festival by storm, rips through Cannes, and then wins an Oscar, at which ceremony you'll step out of an eco-friendly Toyota Prius with a real, live Hollywood starlet on your arm. Flashbulbs popping. The young auteur. In reality, most of us just use our Macs to surf the Internet and send e-mails.

Of course, the mainstream (Mac, Starbucks) has become the outside. There was a time, not too long ago, when people picketed Starbucks. Now Leonard Sweet has an entire book based on the "gospel" according to it (Starbucks). Nowhere is this ethos more apparent than in the object lessons used by Christian authors who work in the narrative nonfiction, "I left my church and found God" genre.

In many ways I have no problem with huge, multinational corporations, even though they've been accused of much corporate evil, including financial excess and abuse of power. Among other contributions, they've enabled the free cell phone that's attached to my ear, they've provided the cheap laptop on which I type, and in some sense they probably provide you with the disposable income that you used to purchase this book.

That said, reading even a cursory sampling of "leave your church" books provides interesting object lessons suggesting that leaving one's church in favor of a revolutionary style of worship is a mostly white, yuppie affectation. The first chapter of Barna's *Revolution* takes place on a golf course. Meanwhile, in his book *Wide Open Spaces*, author Jim Palmer explains that he has left the church in favor of a Wednesday night meeting with a friend at Starbucks. He talks of spiritual discussions on a boat with a best friend. He says of these meetings, "If one of us starts into those religious modes of thinking, or drones on in God-talk that has little correlation to our daily reality, we quickly rein things back in."

And later: "There's no one person or set of persons you can point to as the ones in charge of or responsible for what happens. All of us believe that we have an equal 'calling' to know God and make him known amid ordinary life and people. Everyone is a leader and a follower, everyone is a teacher and a student."[12]

Palmer's construct of "neo-church" certainly sounds exciting, what with regular trips to Starbucks, Panera, and excursions out on his friend's boat. But being involved in these sorts of organic house churches—or for that matter even real church—for any period of time, will reveal that not everyone is a "leader" or "teacher."

Never am I more of a fan of the traditional pastor/flock relationship at our church than when the church has what they call an "unstructured service." The unstructured service is a holdover from the church's freewheeling 1970s days and involves, as you might expect, an open mic where congregants can share a story, pray, or suggest a song. On paper this seems like a great idea. What kind of coldhearted meanie wouldn't be a fan of people sharing encouragement or prayer requests from their heart?

During unstructured services I usually sit and stare at my bulletin, which I've folded into a tiny pile about the size of a square inch. This is nervous energy. Nervous because of the reality that many people weren't gifted with the ability to stand in front of a group and say something that is God-centered, relevant, and brief. Out of the three, I would take brief. Maybe you've been to services like this. You often hear from the sweet older lady who talks for no less than seventeen minutes about her kidney ailment. There is the well-meaning, attractive college guy who shares about how all of the girls in our church's college group want to get physical with him, and how difficult this is. And if you're lucky, you might get a bad poem, because, let's face it, almost all poems are bad.[13] I'm left with the idea that if this is what revolutionary house church would look like on a week-to-week basis, then I'm definitely out.

To be fair, there are always good things that come out of the unstructured service, but I'm usually left feeling really thankful for our pastor and his forty-five-minute expositional sermons. Though it's much sexier to appear to have come up with something off the top of one's head, I'm glad Kevin spends twenty hours each week reading, praying, and preparing his linear sermons.

COMMUNION AT STARBUCKS

In his book *The Gospel According to Starbucks*, Sweet explains that "Starbucks signifies passion and relationship and meaningful experiences," and that "the cup of coffee you enjoy in the morning is much closer to a chalice of communion wine than you realize." He explains that a Starbucks cup "speaks volumes about the significance of what this book is about: a frappuccino faith, a venti[14] life of romance and passion. It's about nothing less than the gospel according to Starbucks."

I've become really averse to "The Gospel according to _____" type-statements. Partly because they're banal and overdone, but partly (mostly, I hope) because the gospel (the real gospel of Christ's death and resurrection) is really important. There should only be one gospel to which we refer. There has been a gospel according to the Simpsons, Patti LaBelle (huh?), The Beatles, Tony Soprano, Bono (of course), Biff Christ's Childhood Pal, Hank Williams, Spider-man, and Neo from the Matrix, among others.

The Starbucks gospel though, according to Sweet, is about the BREW, an acronym (of course) that stands for Being Real Engages the World. And Starbucks, he says, is a realer place than your church, partly because (he says) it's set up to enable and encourage what he calls "soulcafes."

I suppose we all have our opinions on Starbucks. Mine is that I like places like Starbucks because I like the coffee, but I don't necessarily see them as the postmodern town square, church, and community gathering place that Sweet does. I see them as a triumph of modernity. That is, a place where schmucks like me go to pay way more than they should for a cup of coffee. I won't argue that Starbucks isn't comfortable. It is. It's a nice place to read the paper, have a conversation, or listen to Michael Bublé music that has been piped in. But Starbucks wasn't designed to help me have a venti-conversation. It was designed to help me spend venti-dollars. That's okay, but do we really need a "gospel" according to this?

Dan Kimball says "Reading this book [*Gospel According to Starbucks*] is a caffeine jolt. Get ready to be accelerated into the future, with Jesus a central part of the experience." I imagine Jesus in a green apron, asking me if I'd like a scone or an organic chocolate bar to go with my latte and great conversation. Or maybe that's Him behind the Mac, updating His Facebook page.

To read books like Sweet's, Jesus is the guy facilitating the great conversations with your buddies at the coffee shop. He's the guy providing the great sunlight streaming through the trees on the hike you took where you really felt God's presence. And for the record, I have no doubt that this is true. However, He's also the person who reveals Himself in Scripture, and about whom we can know things through Scripture.

GOING TO CHURCH IS NOT A QUAINT WASTE OF TIME, BUT AN ESSENTIAL PART OF A PERSON'S SPIRITUAL LIFE AND GROWTH.

The *Starbucks* book is, of course, a great example of the sort of antiorganized religion book/ethic that is so very popular right now. That's why I'm spending so much time describing it (besides the fact that it's unintentionally hilarious).

According to Sweet, "Most people today don't fret over whether Christianity can get me to heaven. They want to know: Will it make me a better person?" He adds, "The world is not impressed that people attend church on Sunday morning. If anything, such a habit is viewed as a quaint waste of time."

What we're attempting to do is to try to convince you—because people can still try to convince other people of things—that going to heaven is indeed worth fretting about, and going to church is not a quaint waste of time but an important and essential part of a person's spiritual life and growth. In fact, a part that can be real and authentic without trying so painfully hard to be real and authentic.

I, for one, am thankful that I go to a church that isn't trying to be like my coffee shop. I'm glad that someone cares enough about the gospel to preach it to me in a powerful and convincing way. A way that has edges. A way that makes me feel uncomfortable. And I'm thankful that my church doesn't do this to make me feel awkward, unloved, or unwelcomed, rather, for my sanctification and growth.

In *Revolution*, Barna says that he wrote the book to "help Revolution-aries gain a better understanding of themselves," and "crystallize their self-awareness." I would argue that we could do well with a lot less self-awareness, apart from the awareness of our own sinfulness and need for the gospel. We're all too self-aware, as a culture. We can articulate the myriad of ways that our churches and families have failed us. We have whole genres of music dedicated to our personal hurts[15] and wounds.

Hebrews 10:25 declares we should not neglect, "to meet together, as is the habit of some, but encouraging one another, and all the more as you see the Day drawing near." Such interactions, Barna concludes, "could be at a worship service or at Starbucks."[16]

Could it? Will we sing hymns of praise to our God, at Starbucks? Will we pray together, for each other, at Starbucks? Will we be exposed to consistent, biblical, gospel-centered teaching at Starbucks? Perhaps, but I doubt it. And I wonder if the people who are disciplined, motivated, and "type A" enough to make this happen for themselves at Starbucks, have written books that the rest of us can't live up to. For myself, at least, I *need* church. I need the structure of my small-group meeting every other Tuesday or I would probably stop going. I need my accountability e-mail with Cory every Monday, because unlike the illustrations in these books, my life doesn't seem to be a constant stream of mountaintop experiences.

Sweet says that Starbucks "knows that people live for engagement, connection, symbols, and meaningful experiences." I would agree with Sweet on the last statement. But I would argue that people are also looking for truth, and a means by which to worship and learn about the God they claim to follow. And that church can, and still does, provide those means.

NOTES

1. Her quote: "My generation responds to him because he doesn't gloss over life's flaws."
2. I'm typing this at roughly the same time that the latest Batman movie, *The Dark Knight*, hits theaters. Just as in the *Star Wars* saga, expect Christian reviewers to find spiritual significance in the film so as to sort of allow themselves to like it with a clean conscience (see also: U2, and books like *The Gospel According to Tony Soprano*) when they should probably just go ahead and like it anyway.
3. Chris Seay, *The Gospel According to Tony Soprano* (Lake Mary, Fla.: Relevant, 2002), 2.
4. Now I admit I love mob movies like *The Godfather* and *Goodfellas* because of the top-notch writing, great performances, and, to be honest, the romanticizing of the mafia that goes on in them. I think shows like this really touch a chord with wimpy, white suburbanites (like me) because we have no real ethnic heritage and take very few risks in our lives. We're attracted to the strength of characters like Michael Corleone and Henry Hill, even if it's a counterfeit strength and one whose portrayal does leave us feeling dirty and compromised at the end.
5. For example, in *Dear Church* Sarah Cunningham explains that "I seem to dysfunctionally crave edgier life experiences. I've lived and studied in several inner-city areas. . . . I led a

canteen unit at Ground Zero; my husband and I purposefully bought a home in a neighbor-
hood where we would be the clear minority race."

6. The Children in Worship routine is this sort of hippie-ish production that involves, in no
particular order: a feast (usually Goldfish crackers and Dixie cups of water), lighting a candle,
and "a moment of contemplative reflection," which, if you've ever been around five-year-olds,
is absolutely impossible.

7. A friend of mine (male) once described Tim Horton's coffee as "tastes the closest to Folgers."
This was a compliment.

8. Yes, that line is an homage to *What About Bob?* starring Bill Murray.

9. This is "woman" for "had the baby." They say "I went early," meaning I had the baby two
weeks prematurely, like we would say "I went early to Tim Horton's to pick up some coffee
and a doughnut." It's weird.

10. We've all realized, together, that we're trying to do the same thing, which is raise godly
children who love the Lord with all their heart, soul, mind, and strength. We just differ in our
methodology.

11. If you happen to go to my church and are getting uncomfortable reading this section, skip
immediately to the last part of my last chapter (8) for a bunch of positive stuff about our
church.

12. Jim Palmer, *Wide Open Spaces* (Nashville: Thomas Nelson, 2007), 43.

13. I actually like poetry, and my first published works were poems. However, I'm enough of a
realist to know now I'd be mortified if those poems were read aloud somewhere.

14. *Venti* is Italian for *large*, a popular cup size for Starbucks fans.

15. I love Johnny Cash, but if I hear "Hurt" one more time in conjunction with a spiritual
conversation or church service I might lose it.

16. George Barna, *Revolution* (Carol Stream, Ill.: Tyndale, 2005), 114.

Though with a scornful wonder

Men see her sore oppressed,

By schisms rent asunder,

By heresies distressed:

Yet saints their watch are keeping,

Their cry goes up, "How long?"

And soon the night of weeping

Shall be the morn of song!

— "The Church's One Foundation," verse 3

CHAPTER 3

THE PERSONAL:
ON HURT AND HERESY

"Ten Reasons Why Your Church Sucks" is John O'Keefe's colorful contribution to Spencer Burke's latest anthology, *Out of the Ooze: Unlikely Love Letters to the Church Beyond the Pew*.[1] According to O'Keefe, the church is lame (or at least the one his friend left) because it doesn't understand the community, has poor leadership, no vision, is graying quickly, inbred, concerned with appearance over action, comfortable in its misery, out of touch with the times, all about money, and too political.

Others offer different reasons the church is irrelevant. In *They Like Jesus but Not the Church*, Dan Kimball argues that emerging generations can't stand the church because they see it as an organized religion with a political agenda, judgmental and negative, dominated by males and oppressive to females, homophobic, arrogantly claiming all other religions are wrong, and

WHY WE LOVE THE CHURCH

full of fundamentalists who take the whole Bible literally. Similarly, in their research with sixteen-to twenty-nine-year-olds, David Kinnaman and Gabe Lyons found that those outside the church consider Christianity hypocritical, obsessed with conversions, antihomosexual, sheltered, too political, and judgmental.[2] I guess the church has seen better days.

A glutton for punishment, I also read Julia Duin's book *Quitting Church*. In recounting personal conversations with church leaders and church-leavers alike, Duin relates yet more problems with the local church: unhelpful attitudes toward the disabled; lack of support for single moms; paucity of spiritually mature believers; pabulum-puking sermons; shallow, irrelevant preaching; lack of community; unfriendliness toward newcomers; preoccupation with attracting seekers; uncaring church members; and overlooked singles. Add to that shallow doctrine, superficial sexual ethics, limited opportunities for women, abusive pastors, money-hungry pastors, the same old worship services, and passive congregations. The list goes on and on.

THE CHURCH HAS ISSUES

How should we handle these criticisms? Well, it's always a good idea to start by listening. No doubt, every single one of these judgments is right—somewhere and some of the time. There are over 300,000 churches in North America. I'm sure there are more than 300,000 bad experiences and negative impressions to be shared. As Christians, and especially for those of us who are leaders, we need to take an honest look at ourselves and our churches. We all have imbalances. We all have specks to remove, and some of us have planks. We're kidding ourselves if we think our churches don't have weaknesses.

As I read the books mentioned above, I recalled the feedback on my own sermons. Every preacher has to learn to handle criticism. In addition to a lot of encouraging comments, I've been told my sermons are too long, too boring, too light, too heavy, too Reformed, not Reformed enough, too focused on application, and too light on application. A hard-hearted pastor shuts all this out because he's sure anyone who critiques him is a spiritual nincompoop. That's bad. But so is the people-pleasing, damage-control pastor who rewrites the week's message to make Susie-Ticked-Off feel better. I haven't fully figured out how to handle criticism, but first I try to listen and understand what my critics are saying. Then I consider the source—their attitude, their track record, their motives. Finally, I ask the Lord for wisdom to know if I should pay attention or forget about the conversation. That's sort of my approach to "the church stinks" crowd.

I'm sure that the critique fits some churches. I'm sure it misses the mark for others. But the first step is to listen. We may just learn something.

And if we see a fault, let's be quick to admit it. The great preacher Martyn Lloyd-Jones was certainly critical of the idea of churchless Christianity, yet he was quick to acknowledge, "With much of this criticism of the Church one has, of course, to agree. There is so much that is wrong with the Church—traditionalism, formality and

> **AS A PEOPLE, WE'VE CARRIED TOO MUCH SWAGGER AND SHOWN TOO LITTLE BROKENHEARTED HUMILITY.**

lifelessness and so on—and it would be idle and utterly foolish to deny this. . . . The Church so easily can degenerate into an organization, or even, perhaps, a social club or something of that kind; so that it is often necessary to raise the whole question of the Church herself."[3] Some of our churches are dead.

Some of our people *are* mean. No doubt, some of my sermons *are* boring. As a people, we've carried too much swagger and shown too little brokenhearted humility. We've made fun of Mormons, and told gay jokes, and mocked the Clintons. We live in a kooky Christian subculture at times. If someone tells you the church is screwed up, it's certainly true somewhere all of the time and in your neck of the woods some of the time. We must plead with the Lord, "Show me where my church has messed things up. Show me where I've gone off track." There is plenty of blame to go around.

But . . .

You knew there was a "but" coming. I sincerely want us to listen to fair-minded criticism and own up to our share of the blame. Period. Full stop. But church failure is not the whole story. Outsider perceptions are not always accurate, and insider angst is not always fair. Before we write off the church because young nonChristians hate her and thirtysomething church dropouts think she's lame, we need to think more carefully about the critiques. I know it may seem reactionary to criticize the criticisms of the church more than the church itself. I may even look like a defensive pastor trying to protect his turf. But my aim is not to let the church go scot-free for all its mistakes. Instead, I hope to provide some much needed balance and nuance.

Outsiders don't like the church, they say, and insiders like it even less. So clearly the church is totally off-track and out of touch, right? Well . . . not quite.

OUTSIDER PERCEPTIONS

From reading the latest research and from personal experience, I have no doubt that most young people with no connection to the church have a negative impression of the church. On one level, this is a truism. If outsiders thought the church was hot stuff, they would become insiders. So of course outsiders don't like the church. But the statistics are still worth pondering. According to *UnChristian*, 91 percent of outsiders ages sixteen to twenty-nine believe "antihomosexual" describes Christianity "a lot or some." Furthermore, 87 percent think we're judgmental; 85 percent consider Christians hypocritical; and roughly three-fourths think Christians are old-fashioned, out of touch, and insensitive. Almost seven in ten (68 percent) think we're boring, and 64 percent consider Christianity not accepting of other faiths (though it should be noted that these percentages drop considerably if only "a lot" is counted instead of "a lot or some").[4] This is bad news. But the news needs to be balanced by several considerations.

The Young and the Restless

First, the young tend to be the most disillusioned about religion. As Chuck Colson argues in one of the afterwords to *UnChristian*, "We know that historically the youngest generation is impressionable and idealistic. As they mature, they begin to see things that they were hypercritical of in a more mature way. I think people are going to get over their negative views of Christians and will begin to see that Jesus is real. I believe that will happen."[5] Back in 1990, Barna found that then eighteen- to twenty-four-year-olds considered themselves the least religious, followed by twenty-five to thirty-four-year-olds, and then thirty-five to forty-four-year-olds, and so on up the ladder.[6] Carl Henry, writing in the mid-1970s, commented, "Recent surveys show that young people generally hold sharply negative attitudes" concerning "church and religion."[7] This is not surprising. Younger generations are almost always less interested in church and religion. Since at least the 1960s, young people in this country have questioned whatever is old, big, and institutional, and been into whatever seems different, independent, and novel. This combination of tastes means that historic faith will usually seem suspect to young people outside the church.

On a related note, the claim that people like Jesus but not church is worth almost nothing in my estimation. Even Dan Kimball in his book *They*

Like Jesus but Not the Church recognizes that what outsiders like is a pop-culture Jesus.[8] If outsiders are into Jesus, we'd be foolish not to use that as a starting place, but we're kidding ourselves if we think most nonChristians (or Christians for that matter) have any idea who Jesus really was and the claims He made. Karen Ward, an emergent church leader in Seattle, claims that 95 percent of the nonchurched in her area have a favorable view of Jesus, "so Jesus is not the problem. It is the church they dislike, because they do not readily see the church living out his teachings."[9] But the Jesus they like is almost certainly not the Jesus who calls sinners to repentance, claimed to be the unique Son of God, and died for our sins. He is almost certainly a nice guy, open-minded, spiritually ambiguous, and a good example. He is guru Jesus who resembles Bono in a bathrobe. If the church is the problem, it is likely because the church gives shape and form to an otherwise malleable and hollow Christ.

Virtual Reality

Second, perceptions are not always reality. Gabe Lyons, coauthor of *UnChristian*, maintains that "to assume that the six major labels that David [Kinnaman] described are merely misperceptions of Christians would be a huge mistake. These perceptions are based on real experiences that outsiders have had with their Christian friends. They are an accurate reflection of the kind of Christians many of us have become. It's embarrassing and shameful, but it's reality."[10] This statement is, of course, true. Many Christians are bozos. But many more are not. Some of the church's bad press is deserved. Some is not. It takes humility and discernment for each church and each Christian to determine if they are part of the problem or just being faithful.

The polls are useful to a point. They give us clues as to where our blindspots might be. But the blindness might not always be ours. I know it sounds like a convenient out, but 2 Corinthians 4:4 is still true: "The god of this world has blinded the minds of unbelievers." I'm not surprised that defending biblical marriage looks antigay to nonChristians. I'm not shocked that outsiders think Christians are antiscience because they believe in a Creator God. Of course, we sometimes add to our own problems with too much bluster and too few facts, but we must remember that there will always be aspects of our faith that are unpopular. As Elton Trueblood said years ago:

> People naturally resist the conception of an objective moral order, finding it far more comfortable to suppose that all moral laws have only subjective reference and can therefore be neglected with impunity. We are missing the point terribly if we do not see that a faith which is as definite as the Gospel of Christ is now and always will be a stone of stumbling and an occasion of offense. Because the sharp line is never popular, we are foolish to expect it to be so. Those who try to follow the narrow way must expect to be part of the minority all of their lives."[11]

Anticipating this kind of rebuttal, Kinnaman is quick to point out that he doesn't want a hijacked Jesus who is an openhearted, never-offending, good moral teacher.[12] This is heartening. Having met David Kinnaman, I know he doesn't want to sell out or water down the gospel just to make it palatable. But we need to be careful with our Christianese euphemisms that they don't end up distorting the gospel. Elsewhere Kinnaman describes "a more complete picture of Jesus" as a "transcendent yet personal God who loves and accepts you perfectly, who wants to shape you and give your life deep meaning and purpose. This is the Jesus I want to describe, even if the actions and attitudes of Christ followers have not always represented this to you."[13] I commend Kinnaman for trying to reach nonChristians with this

WHY WE LOVE THE CHURCH

language, but hasn't this "more complete picture of Jesus" shaved off all the sharp edges of the gospel? No one will be offended by a transcendent yet personal god who accepts us perfectly and wants to give our lives meaning and purpose. But this is not the Jesus the apostles preached. Their Jesus was transcendent and personal, but He warned of judgment and demanded repentance. He spoke freely of sin, salvation, and the necessity of new birth. The apostles preached Christ dead, buried, and raised for our justification. They preached Christ and Him alone. They told of all that God had accomplished in Christ for miserable sinners. That was their message and the world hated them for it.

How Despicable

Third, the church has often been despised. It would be wrong to wear unpopularity as a sure marker of faithfulness. But by the same token, we should not assume we have failed just because outsiders dislike us. It is well known that the Romans despised the early Christians. They were considered odd, unlearned, ungodly, culturally lowbrow, and socially unprofitable. The Romans thought the Christians practiced cannibalism because they ate the body and drank the blood of Jesus. Some thought they were incestuous because they called each other brother and sister and took part in love feasts. Others thought they were atheists because they had no icons for their God.

"Whether or not the Christians merited these three charges of atheism, incest and cannibalism is beside the point," argues Michael Green in his book *Evangelism in the Early Church*. "They were universally regarded as the sort of people who might be guilty of crimes like these. Their early press was uniformly bad."[14]

It can be helpful to know how others perceive us, but not always. In our self-esteem-oriented, easily offended, suffering-averse world, I fear that the

80

church is too eager to be liked. "As we study the New Testament," suggests Trueblood, "we soon realize that part of the power of the early Christian Movement arose from the clear recognition that it was by no means popular or generally accepted. The hope of reaching the masses with a redemptive power was always prefaced by the clear recognition that the opposition was intense as well as abundant."[15] Of course Christianity has an "image problem."[16] At times, this is our own fault. But at other times, our lack of an image problem has been just as damning. We've been indistinct from the world with nothing to set us apart, nothing to

> **PEOPLE'S RECEPTION TO THE GOSPEL IS ALWAYS A MIXED BAG. PAUL WAS HONORED AND DISHONORED, SLANDERED AND PRAISED.**

suggest a transformed life or renewed thinking bound by the Word of God. We've lusted after academic recognition and cultural validation. We've fancied ourselves fashionable and looked around for the world to take notice.

The answer is not a return to fundamentalist obscurantism. The answer is a clean conscience before God. "But with me it is a very small thing that I should be judged by you or by any human court. In fact, I do not even judge myself. I am not aware of anything against myself, but I am not thereby acquitted. It is the Lord who judges me" (1 Cor. 4:3–4). Elsewhere Paul writes, "We put no obstacle in anyone's way, so that no fault may be found with our ministry" (2 Cor. 6:3). We need to get on our faces before God and ask Him to show us our sin. Where there is sin, we need to repent. Where there isn't, we need to keep doing church whether it makes us popular or not.

Strangely enough, the ministry so nicely executed by Paul still resulted in afflictions, beatings, imprisonments, riots, and calamities (6:4–5). People's reception to the gospel is always a mixed bag. Paul was honored and dishonored, slandered and praised (6:8). "We are treated as impostors, and yet are true; as unknown, and yet well known; as dying, and behold, we live; as punished, and yet not killed; as sorrowful, yet always rejoicing; as poor, yet making many rich; as having nothing, yet possessing everything" (6:8–10). He might say today: "as having an image problem, and yet living out the image of God; as despised, yet never despairing." Being disliked by teenagers and twentysomethings is not our biggest problem. To quote Andy Crouch, whose gently critical remarks are included in *UnChristian*: "I'm not eager for us to manage perceptions of Christians, Christianity, or Christ. Jesus, thankfully, doesn't need our spin control."[17]

INSIDER ANGST

We can understand outsiders being unhappy with the church, but why are Christians sick of it? In a way, that's the subject of this whole book. But in the rest of this chapter I want to look at the question more existentially. Some church-leavers could probably articulate a coherent theological-missiological-historical case for their disillusionment with the church. But more are leaving because of sheer personal exhaustion. They just don't like church anymore.

For starters, *they think church is boring*. The sermons are either too long and dogmatic or too breezy and superficial. Either way, they're dull. The worship is formulaic. The services are monotonous. The routines are, well, routine.

Second, they are tired of the outdated Christian subculture. It's no coincidence that after the boomer generation in the 1980s and 1990s successfully connected with the church, today's young adults—born twenty-five years later—often feel left out. The church imbibed one generation's tastes, only to find that their offspring want to spit it out of their mouths. It's one thing for the church to feel like a time warp that sends you back one hundred, five hundred, or fifteen hundred years. It's another thing completely if the time warp brings you back to 1990. The church tried too hard to be relevant a generation ago and now we are paying the price.

Third, church-leavers hate the megachurch. They view their old seeker churches with unreserved contempt. They disdain the parking lot attendants with orange vests and the ubiquitous greeters around every corner. In their experience, church is where a lot of people show up and don't do anything, where evangelism and the seeker are all that matter, where every Sunday must be a celebration, where suburbia is king, where pastors are godlike CEOs, where another building is always under construction and another capital campaign is coming soon. This depiction may seem to lack charity, but this is what many people have known (or think they have known) as church the past couple of decades.

Fourth, disgruntled insiders feel like church is abusive. We could fill stadiums with people hurt by the church, says one church-leaver.[18] Another claims to know "churches and church people who have imprisoned and messed up people with oppressive legalism and fear-based obedience to God."[19] Church abuse does not mean physical harm or even verbal tirades. Abuse, for the church-is-lame crowd, occurs when you have to accept the word of those in authority, when someone claims to speak the Word of God without reference to the wider community, when decisions are made in secret by a small group, when difference is demonized, and when control is exercised to maintain the institution.[20] As one former churchgoer puts it, "Church abuse" exists "when pastors and members think they are better than you and strive to beat you—spiritually and emotionally—into thinking like them."[21]

Fifth, the church seems inauthentic. People are just going through the motions, according to many church insiders. The smiles are as fake as the designer shoes. Greeting-card theology passes for spiritual meat. Doubt and suffering are embarrassments. The church just isn't real. Tony Jones tells the story of Brett who hates the church because when he was recovering from an injury and in a great deal of pain and loneliness, church people told him to just have more faith in Jesus or trust the Bible and everything would be better. But the two things that kept him alive were not Jesus and the Bible but his infant daughter and Prozac. The message Brett heard was that God will magically alleviate the symptoms of life-crushing depression if we just believe. This kind of quick-fix, pain-free phoniness "sucked the spiritual life from his veins" until he finally gave up on church.[22]

CAUTION FOR THE CRITICS

It would be foolish for me to try to refute people's individual experiences with the church. As I've said already, no question, some people have been hurt by bad churches. But I'd like church-leavers to consider that some of their angst may be self-induced and some of their pain is more personal than profound. That is to say, it's possible that a good deal of the problem for church-leavers rests with the one leaving and not just the church.

In all honesty I can say that in the times I've been hurt by church people or been disheartened, the biggest problems, in the end, proved to be those that came from my own heart. This is not to discount external pressures or difficult situations or the ways in which Christians can hurt each other. Yet even with all these outside factors, my main issue has been Kevin. I respond in sinful ways. I feel sorry for myself. I lose faith. I doubt the Word of God. I don't want to forgive. I stop hoping. I get embittered. I grow lazy. I don't stay in step with the Spirit. These are *my* sins from *my* heart. Others can make life difficult for me. I can make it unbearable.

So before the disgusted and dismayed write off the church, I'd like to wave a large caution flag in the form of four questions.

FOUR QUESTIONS FOR THE CHURCH-LEAVER

1. Are you rejecting the church or the faith?

There's a disturbing trend in many of the church-leaver books. People are not just getting bored with church. They are rejecting the historic Christian faith.

Take William P. Young, for example. Young is the author of *The Shack*, the surprise bestseller that started out as a simple story for his kids and has now sold millions of copies. Young, like his friend Wayne Jacobsen who published the book, are no longer a part of the institutional church. They say they have found Jesus in more depth and more freedom outside the walls of organized religion. In watching some interviews with Young, I'm struck by his sincerity. He seems a kind man, one who didn't set out to write a theologically controversial book. But after reading *The Shack*, I conclude that Young has rejected more than just the church. He has rejected evangelical Christianity and historic orthodoxy.

In telling the story of Mack's (the book's main character) encounter with the Trinity in an old shack in the woods, Young introduces us to God the Father as a big, black woman named Papa, God the Son as a Jewish man with a big nose, and God the Spirit as a woman of Asian extraction named Sarayu. Young's God is a God who is especially fond of everyone everywhere and loves everyone in the same way,[23] a God who doesn't punish people for sin (because sin is its own punishment).[24] There is no order or authority in this God. The Father submits to Jesus just as Jesus submits to the Father. In fact, God even submits to us.[25] In Young's theology, evil and darkness do not really exist, but are just the absence of goodness and light.[26]

I could keep going with the theological problems in *The Shack*. In Young's thinking, the old heresy of patripassianism (the Father suffering with the Son on the cross) is revived, God's sovereignty over suffering is rejected, and all human beings are already reconciled to God (we just need to choose to live in the relationship).[27] Most troubling of all, in an attempt to depict a warm, loving deity, Young has made God into a chummy, sometimes stern, but never awe-inspiring, drop-on-my-knees-as-though-dead kind of Lord. Mack doesn't cry out "Woe is me" in the presence of this God or fall on his face into a pile of smelly fish in reverent fear. He swears and complains.[28] This God is more "hang out" than holy. I don't doubt that many hurting people have found comfort in *The Shack*. But the depiction of the Christian faith in *The Shack* is not simply a little off here or there. It is a deviation from the historic faith in many, and important, places.

Spencer Burke is another former pastor who has left the church. His faith commitment is even sketchier. Burke rejects the need for conversion, the idea of hell, and the notion that the atonement was a sacrifice for sin.[29] Faith is not necessary, God is not personal, and spiritual life is defined as a commitment to personal, social, and communal transformation.[30]

A final example can be found in Jim Palmer, who has "pioneered a unique expression of 'church' as a social network of people."[31] Palmer decries the usual focus on Christ as a historical figure (always a bad sign), and instead is interested in Christ "the life-giving-spirit within."[32] He defines faith as "believing that what you are experiencing is God."[33] Truth is what helps me experience freedom.[34] God, for Palmer, is defined most of all by unconditional acceptance[35] He is everything, the sum total of all that exists, "an intimate, loving, caring, life-giving energy or spirit" that is "the root of all living things."[36]

There's no nice way to say it: This is not Christianity. We could call it Palmerism, a new "experience God yourself" religion.

Before the unhappy masses exit the church, they should consider what it is they are actually leaving. Is it merely some bad experiences they are fleeing? Or does the unrest go deeper? If Christians are interested in a Christianity free from doctrine, demands, and damnation, they aren't just sick of the church and its unflattering quirks; they're tired of the Christian faith altogether.

2. Are you trying to have your cake and eat it too?

"You can't have your cake and eat it too" has to be one of the most confusing aphorisms. *Why can't I have my cake and eat it too?* I've often thought. What else do you do once you have cake except eat it? But "have" in the saying is more like "keep." You can't eat your cake and still expect to keep it. It's one or the other.

I mention this aphorism because it fits many contemporary church critics. They leave the institutional church with its buildings and programs and paid staff and go to serve at the homeless shelter instead, never stopping to think that someone pays the bills for this building, someone turns on the heat in the morning, and someone maintains a calendar of events every month. The church-leavers can feel good tithing to the nonprofit of their choice, never stopping to think that this superspiritual, supercool outfit has a board of directors and an accountant, and filed the paperwork to become a 501c3 back in the day. I'm not against homeless shelters or parachurch nonprofits. I just want the anti-institutional church-leavers to see that these are institutions too.

> THEY [CHURCH CRITICS] WANT LEADERS WITH VISION BUT DON'T WANT ANYONE TO TELL THEM WHAT TO DO OR HOW TO THINK.

But then again, consistency is not a postmodern virtue. And nowhere is this more aptly displayed than in the barrage of criticisms leveled against the church. The church-is-lame crowd hates Constantine and notions of

Christendom, but they want the church to be a patron of the arts, and run after-school programs, and bring the world together in peace and love. They bemoan the over-programmed church, but then think of a hundred complex, resource-hungry things the church should be doing. They don't like the church because it is too hierarchical, but then hate it when it has poor leadership. They wish the church could be more diverse, but then leave to meet in a coffee shop with other well-educated thirtysomethings who are into film festivals, NPR, and carbon offsets. They want more of a family spirit, but too much family and they'll complain that the church is "inbred." They want the church to know that its reputation with outsiders is terrible, but then are critical when the church is too concerned with appearances. They chide the church for not doing more to address social problems, but then complain when the church gets too political.[37] They want church unity and decry all our denominations, but fail to see the irony in the fact that they have left to do their own thing because they can't find a single church that can satisfy them.[38] They are critical of the lack of community in the church, but then want services that allow for individualized worship experiences.[39] They want leaders with vision, but don't want anyone to tell them what to do or how to think. They want a church where the people really know each other and care for each other, but then they complain the church today is an isolated country club, only interested in catering to its own members.[40] They want to be connected with history, but are sick of the same prayers and same style every week. They call for not judging "the spiritual path of other believers who are dedicated to pleasing God and blessing people," and then they blast the traditional church in the harshest, most unflattering terms.[41]

They'd like to have their cake and eat it too.

3. Are you making an idol out of authenticity?

The Bible is all for honesty, truth, and sincerity, but authenticity is something a little different. If authentic is simply the opposite of fake, contrived, and hypocritical, then I'm all for it. I like people who are honest with their feelings and open about their struggles. But godliness demands a lot more than just being real. In fact, godliness demands that we stop acting like we want to and start acting like Christ. I sometimes find, especially among my peers, that authenticity is not a self-abasing means of growing in holiness, but a convenient cover for endless introspection, doubt, uncertainty, anger, and worldliness. So that if other Christians seem pure, assured, and happy, we despise them for being inauthentic.

Granted, the church shouldn't be happy-clappy naive about life's struggles. Plenty of psalms show us godly ways to be real with our negative emotions. But the church should not apologize for preaching a confident Christ and exhorting us to trust Him in all things. Church is not meant to foster an existential crisis of faith every week, nor are we justified in leaving church because there seem to be too many answers offered to our questions. Belief is not the enemy of authenticity.

In *Divine Nobodies*, Jim Palmer talks about his friend Bill, whose wife died tragically in a horse riding accident. To Palmer's shock, Bill insisted he was not angry with God. "In disbelief, I would often think, *Come on, Bill. Be real. She's not even my wife, and I'm angry and disillusioned with God.*"[42] To Palmer's credit he admits to rewriting part of the chapter because Bill felt like he (Bill) came across disillusioned when that really wasn't the case. Bill explains,

> And finally, in the next to last paragraph, I would have to say your
> questions outlined were really not questions I had. I know you are
> trying not to have pat Christian answers to hard questions in cir-

cumstances like these, but somehow, I never really wondered, for example, if God killed Carol Ann. I wondered why he allowed it, but I always knew there was some reason I would never know and didn't care to know really. His ways were beyond my understanding, and I knew it. I always knew he was good, just that my circumstances were not, and reconciling that was difficult. I remember early on, rarely feeling abandoned, often feeling his presence, but at the same time feeling deep pain, which again was difficult to reconcile. I wasn't angry, just very confused. There is a big difference, and I couldn't really own the words of that paragraph.[43]

Palmer eventually grows to respect his friend's faith and learn from it, but it's telling (and authentic I suppose) that he found such trust "baffling and vexing."[44] I know Christians can be impatient with sufferers and expect them to "move on" after a few prayers and couple minutes with Romans 8:28. That's not the way to care for people. But let's not be professional cynics either. We are meant to be comforted by Jesus and the Bible is supposed to help. We should trust God and not be angry with Him. We should not consider ourselves abandoned. This is not phony Christianity; it's faith. And it's the kind of sensitive, mature Christianity we should be glad for in our churches.

4. Are you repeating the mistakes of the previous generation?

Clearly, a growing number of Christians don't like the church. The church doesn't work for them anymore. And, by their reasoning, if the church doesn't work for you, then the best thing to do is just leave. When an acquaintance challenged Palmer on not going to church anymore, Palmer decided not to accept his challenge because the thought of worshiping God in the confines of organized church didn't pass his "freedom filter."[45] Likewise,

Barna asks, "Does something get in the way of your living like Jesus? Then figure out how to eliminate the obstruction."[46] And fellow church-leaver Wayne Jacobsen writes: "Periodically on this journey we may go through times when we can't seem to find any other believers who share our hunger. That's especially true for those who find that conforming to the expectations of the religious institutions around them diminishes their relationship with Jesus."[47]

The logic here is pretty simple. If by your estimation church does not help you know God better, than you stop going to church.[48] In fact, "Continuing to attend a religious service or event after you have long since decided that event or program actually keeps you from authentic encounter with God is hypocrisy."[49]

But what if belonging to the church is more serious than, say, choosing whether the new laundry detergent is "right for you"? What if your difficulty with church was God's means of sanctifying you and the church, instead of separating the two of you? What if we aren't always the best judge of what will help us most in "living like Jesus"? What if, in addition to the church, we feel like marriage "diminishes" our relationship with Jesus? Or that poverty doesn't seem to be good for us spiritually? Or our children get in the way of our walk with God? What if we need something to guide us that is more sophisticated, more sure, and less subjective than our own "freedom filters"? And what makes us think that after nearly two thousand years of institutional church, Christians are suddenly free to jettison the church and try things on their own?

DISILLUSIONMENT WITH THE CHURCH IS NOT NEW.

This isn't the first time Christians have been tired of the church. Back in the 1960s and 70s, the Jesus People were fed up with institutional religion too. They were not unlike today's Disgruntled Johnnys and Janets. They had evangelistic zeal and didn't see any in the church. They were committed to small-group Bible study and prayer and found them lacking elsewhere. They were more in touch with their brokenness and wanted the church to do more to speak to societal problems. The Jesus People movement was a reaction against what they perceived to be dead orthodoxy in the church and a preoccupation with political concerns (although on the left instead of the right). The movement was not all bad, not by a long shot. They wanted more passion in the church and more commitment. They lamented the fact that ecclesiastical bureaucracy was often a mask for spiritual lethargy.

But the movement was also "vulnerable to doctrinal inconsistencies and spiritual imbalance." Most in the Jesus People movement tended to be mono-generational, hyperexperiential and antihistorical.[50] They could be "intellectually shallow and doctrinally tolerant," accommodating sub-biblical and even heretical concepts for the sake of "Christian love."[51] They were susceptible to personality cults and fads, and their utopian communes did not prove to be the family of the future.[52] Most in the Jesus People movement eventually faded back into the church, and a few left Christianity completely.

The point is this: Disillusionment with the church is not new. The frustration and impatience with the church are not new either. The church has a habit of being slow to learn, but if the Spirit is blowing in the new winds, she will learn her lesson, even if often she forgets it again.

So I am not worried for the church. She will survive the latest revolution. Her services, her sermons, her institutional form will not disappear.

However, I am worried for church-leavers. I wonder if they will be happy in five years with their new form of church. I wonder if they will keep up the revolution without the life-support of structure and routine. I wonder if they will escape their own cynicism and anger. Most of all I worry that in leaving the church they are leaving the faith of the church and the Christ of two thousand years of church history. I feel sorry for their hurts and worry about their hearts.

NOTES

1. Spencer Burke, comp., *Out of the Ooze:* (Colorado Springs, NavPress, 2007), 179–83.

2. David Kinnaman and Gabe Lyons, *UnChristian* (Grand Rapids: Baker, 2007).

3. D. Martyn Lloyd-Jones, *Preaching and Preachers* (Grand Rapids: Zondervan, 1972), 10.

4. Kinnaman and Lyons, *UnChristian*, 28.

5. As quoted in Kinnaman and Lyons, *UnChristian*, 236.

6. George Barna, *The Frog in the Kettle* (Ventura, Calif.: Regal 1990), 161.

7. Carl F. H. Henry, *God, Revelation, and Authority,* vol. 1 (1976; repr. 1999 Wheaton, Ill.: Crossway), 132.

8. Dan Kimball, *They Like Jesus but Not the Church* (Grand Rapids, Zondervan, 2007), 55, 255–56.

9. Quoted in Eddie Gibbs and Ryan Bolger, *Emerging Churches: Creating Christian Community in Postmodern Cultures* (Grand Rapids: Baker, 2005), 48.

10. Kinnaman and Lyons, *UnChristian*, 222.

11. Elton Trueblood, *The Incendiary Fellowship* (New York: Harper and Row, 1967), 25.

12. Kinnaman and Lyons, *UnChristian*, 33.

13. Ibid., 20.

14. Michael Green, *Evangelism in the Early Church*, Revised Edition (1970; repr. Grand Rapids: Eerdmans, 2003), 64.

15. Trueblood, *Incendiary Fellowship*, 15.

16. As quoted in Kinnaman and Lyons, *UnChristian,* 11.

17. As quoted in Kinnaman and Lyons, *UnChristian*, 230.

18. Brian Sanders, *Life After Church:* (Downers Grove, Ill.: InterVarsity, 2007), 33

19. Jim Palmer, *Divine Nobodies* (Nashville: W Publishing, 2006), 27.

20. Andy Morgan, "The Paradox of a Divide Church Called to Be Reconcilers to the World" in Burke, *Out of the Ooze*, 77.

21. John O'Keefe, "Ten Reasons Why Your Church Sucks" in Burke, *Out of the Ooze*, 179.

22. Tony Jones, *The New Christians: Dispatches from the Emergent Frontier* (San Francisco: Jossey-Bass, 2008), 172.

23. William P. Young, *The Shack:* (Los Angeles: Windblown, 2007), 118–19.

24. Ibid., 120.

25. Ibid., 122, 145.

26. Ibid., 136.

27. Ibid., 164, 165, 225, respectively.

28. Ibid., 140.

29. Spencer Burke and Barry Taylor, *Heretic's Guide to Eternity* (San Francisco: Jossey-Bass, 2006), 197, 199, and 64–65, respectively.

30. Ibid., 184–88, 195, and 211, respectively.

31. Jim Palmer, *Wide Open Spaces: Beyond Paint-by-Number Christianity* (Nashville: Thomas Nelson, 2007), back cover.

32. Ibid., 19.

33. Ibid., 23.

34. Ibid., 139.

35. Ibid., 49.

36. Ibid., 168, 171.

37. See, for example, Burke, *Out of the Ooze*, 179–83.

38. See Sarah Cunningham, *Dear Church* (Grand Rapids: Zondervan, 2006), 103.

39. See George Barna, *Revolution* (Carol Stream, Ill.: Tyndale, 2005), 62.

40. See Cunningham, *Dear Church*, 180.

41. See Barna, *Revolution*, 20, 114ff. Barna tries to preempt criticism of his revolutionaries by encouraging Christians to bless and not judge, especially their spiritual kinfolk (138, 140). Yet *Revolution* is, among other things, a judgment on the way we currently do church. One gets the impression after reading Barna that regular church folk are benighted at best and woefully immature at worst.

42. Palmer, *Divine Nobodies*, 122.

43. Ibid., 123.

44. Ibid.

45. Palmer, *Wide Open Spaces*, 144–46.

46. Barna, *Revolution*, 26.

47. Wayne Jacobsen, "Why I Don't Go to Church Anymore!", 183. This article is an appendix in *So You Don't Want to Go to Church Anymore: An Unexpected Journey* (Los Angeles: Windblown Media, 2006), written by Wayne Jacobsen and Dave Coleman under the pseudonym Jake Colsen.

48. See Colsen, *So You Don't Want to Go to Church Anymore*, 35.

49. Sanders, *Life After Church*, 5.

50. Henry, *God, Revelation, and Authority*, 126.

51. Ibid., 132.

52. Ibid., 133–34.

You have a class of young, strong men and women,

and they want to give their lives to something.

Advertising has these people chasing cars and clothes

they don't need. . .We don't have a great war in our

generation, or a great depression, but we do have

a great war of the spirit. We have a great revolution

against the culture. The great depression is our lives.

We have a spiritual depression.

– The Mechanic, *Fight Club* (the book)

"I ask you what you think of the faithful minister

of Christ, who honestly exposes sin and pricks your

conscience. Mind how you answer that question.

Too many, nowadays, like only those ministers who

prophesy smooth things and let their sins alone,

who flatter their pride and amuse their intellectual

taste, but who never sound an alarm, and never

tell them of a wrath to come."

– J. C. Ryle, *Holiness*

CHAPTER 4

APPETITE FOR DECONSTRUCTION:
WHY CHURCH IS BORING, CHRISTIANS ARE (INSERT: LAME, CLOSE– MINDED, OR CLIQUISH), AND THE CHURCH DOESN'T CARE ABOUT (INSERT: MY ISSUE). WHY ALL OF THIS IS BOTH TRUE AND UNTRUE.

Writing at 6:41 a.m. from a college dormitory at Moody Bible Institute. This is my first full-fledged extended speaking gig, as Kevin DeYoung and I are speaking twice a day in an auditorium here on campus about *Why We're Not Emergent*. The workmanlike-ness of this section comes from general exhaustion, travel-lag, and a Lunesta-induced fog (see: sleeping in college dormitory with a pillow as thick as a gauze pad).

We are at a pastors' conference—sort of like church camp for adult men. There are workshops, meals, name tags, a comedian, a praise band, and even a snack time in the evening where two thousand of us pad down to the commons area to collect a cookie and a can of pop before bed. We can even stay up late and watch the latest in bad Christian movies (this time, *Fireproof*).[1]

But on to the excellent part. I have had the privilege of hearing Keith and

Kristyn Getty lead worship, which constitutes the first time, in all honesty, I've ever been excited about anyone leading worship. I'm just not the kind of guy to get really cranked up over worship music. The real treat though, has been hearing Albert Mohler and Alistair Begg preach the gospel and, specifically, preach to pastors about the importance of expository (verse by verse) preaching in a culture that doesn't seem to want to have anything to do with being taught propositional truths.

PASSIONATE, FUNNY, AND GOSPEL-CENTERED

Watching these men work is like watching any of the handful of people in the world who are truly "world class" do what they do. I felt the same way watching Michael Jordan play basketball in person. I knew I was in the presence of true, God-given talent. Mohler and Begg are passionate, prepared, funny when appropriate, challenging, and gospel-centered. They have a passion for the Bible and I felt blessed to sit under their biblical teaching, even for a few hours. As a non-pastor here, I feel like the proverbial fly on the wall.

"How likely are you to hear an explicitly expository message from the Word of God coming from an evangelical pulpit?" asks Mohler in his first talk. "The sad thing is that this is no longer just the expectation. The fact that there is a question in our minds should tell us something about the crisis that is looming in our midst. Is it more likely or less likely? One of the challenges we face is that there are some who are telling preachers to do almost anything other than the exposition of the Scriptures. You have to wonder, when you look at a crisis like this, if it's by some kind of strategy. I would suggest that it is.

"The exposition of the Scriptures should be the easiest thing in the world to understand. As a matter of fact, you have to be clever to mess it up." He then gives a short course in homiletics from the book of Nehemiah, which he basically sums up thusly: "Read and explain."

"How do we mess this up? This isn't *The Ezra Code*. You don't have to decipher some hidden meaning. Here's how it works. You read and explain, you read and explain, you read and explain. Then you go home and take a nap."

But Mohler goes on to explain a little bit about the man, Ezra, doing the preaching. We learn that he was "skilled in the law of Moses" (Ezra 7:6), he was "learned in the words of the commandments of the Lord" (7:11), and that the "hand of the Lord his God was upon him" (7:6 all NASB). "This speaks to calling (v.6), as well as talent and training (v. 6 and 11).

"But there will be a generation of itching ears who will want anything other than the preaching of the Word. This Word that is living and active and sharper than any double-edged sword . . . when it is let loose it messes up our lives. It does what not another message can do. It does what no therapy can do. It conforms us to the image of Christ. Paul informs us that we are to do this, continuously."

Also cool: I met Al Mohler in the hallway and he had heard of my book. He's the president of the Southern Baptist Theological Seminary, has about nine book projects going at the moment (all sound amazing), and writes a great blog at www.albertmohler.org.

Meeting Some Pastors

The pastors' conference was an eye-opening experience for me, a non-pastor. I got to spend a week having really interesting conversations with a whole bunch of mostly hardworking, earnest, kind pastors who are really concerned about shepherding their flocks and reaching them with the gospel.

Having read more bad books over the course of the last year, both as research for this book and for *Why We're Not Emergent*, I had settled into a sort of de facto, either/or dynamic in which pastors are either wanna-be revolutionary types, or mostly boring but get-the-gospel-right young Reformed types. What I see here, at the conference, is a "both" situation. These guys, for the most part, are real and passionate about worship, about getting the gospel right,[2] and about reaching the lost. They sincerely care about reaching postmoderns, and not just because their future (read: numbers) depends on it. Most of them have been to seminary, and while seminary, as all of the "left the church and found God" books will tell you, isn't in any way a fast track to superspirituality,[3] the majority of these men have spent more time studying the Scriptures and classic Christian texts than I have. I appreciate them for this. I'm reminded of 2 Timothy 2:2, which reads, "And what you have heard from me in the presence of many witnesses entrust to faithful men who will be able to teach others also." This would suggest that there is a good deposit whose future Paul felt was important enough to entrust to qualified men. This would suggest that pastors are something more than conversation partners. The fact that they think they can learn something from me is incredibly humbling and, to be honest, a little terrifying.

They've also committed their lives to an enterprise (church) which can largely feel like a losing, uphill battle, and the Bible tells us will be out of place and largely reviled in culture. A lot of them feel discouraged and look tired.

Periods of Disgruntledness

But I also appreciate the fact that these guys aren't unwilling to critique their own institutions. In a roundtable discussion with pastors (some of which takes place online, and some in person), many of them express periods of "disgruntledness" with the church, in their own lives.

"Most of it had to do with leadership either not taking stands or being too narcissistic," explains Mike Hess, a pastor from St. Louis. "But I'm looking for a church that faithfully, zealously, and consistently preaches the Word in an expository fashion, is willing to kick me out if I am not living right (church discipline), and one that is not addicted to pragmatism" (read "church marketing").

Hess's picture of the church, and indeed the one painted in Scripture, looks less like our heavily-marketed country clubs, and more like a battle front. Church, while a place of fellowship and friendship, is also the place we go to train and prepare for war.[4] Consider this challenge by J. C. Ryle, to all of the lukewarm, bored, apathetic churchgoers of his day (1850s):

> For another thing, let me warn all careless members of churches to beware lest they trifle their souls into hell. You live on year after year as if there was no battle to be fought with sin, the world, and the devil. You pass through life a smiling, laughing, gentlemanlike or ladylike person, and behave as if there was no devil, no heaven and no hell. Oh, careless churchman, or careless dissenter,[5] careless Episcopalian, careless Presbyterian,[6] careless Independent, careless Baptist, awake to see eternal realities in their true light! Awake and put on the armor of God! Awake and fight hard for life! Tremble, tremble and repent.[7]

THE CHURCH, CONCENTRATION, AND THE BOXER

More than anything, the above quote speaks to the church's importance and to use an overused term—relevance. Except that "relevance" isn't a posture you affect that has more to do with lights, music, candles, mystery, or space than with the gospel. Church, to us, should be as relevant as the gym is to the boxer, or as basic training is to the soldier. We wouldn't go into a fight without training or thinking about our strategy.

A few summers ago I trained as a boxer, mostly so that I could experience what the fighters experienced who I interviewed for my first book, *Facing Tyson*. I had never concentrated harder in my life than when I was in the ring, alone, with another guy who wanted nothing more than to knock me unconscious. This is a whole new level of commitment, dedication, and single-mindedness. I heard and saw nothing outside of the shuffling of feet on canvas, my opponent's breathing,

CHURCH IS BORING BECAUSE WE NEUTER IT OF ITS IMPORTANCE.

and the few inches of peripheral vision outside my headgear. Concentration was relevant.

Church isn't boring because we're not showing enough film clips, or because we play an organ instead of a guitar. It's boring because we neuter it of its importance. Too often we treat our spiritual lives like the round of golf used to open George Barna's *Revolution*. At the end of my life, I want my friends and family to remember me as someone who battled for the gospel, who tried to mortify sin in my life, who fought hard for life, and who contended earnestly for the faith. Not just as a nice guy who occasionally noticed the splendor of the mountains God created, while otherwise just trying to enjoy myself, manage my schedule, and work on my short game.

APPETITE FOR DECONSTRUCTION

Conferences like this give a person a lot of time to reflect on Christian culture. We see, among other things, a Christian comedian, a Christian painter, and a couple of Christian movies during the course of the week. Kevin and I spend a lot of time ruminating on the idea that people who aren't necessarily paid to/trying to be funny, like Mohler and Begg, often end up being a lot funnier than the guy who was brought in to make us laugh in a clean, family-friendly way. Mohler and Begg are funny because their jokes cut to the quick of many prominent issues in evangelical culture.

And you already probably know what I think about Christian movies. I have a theory about Christian movies and kids who attend upscale, Christian liberal arts colleges.[8] My theory is that if you are exposed to, say, thirty seconds of a "Christian" movie, you immediately know you're watching a Christian movie without necessarily being told up front. They all have a "look." It's something inherent in the lighting, the way the actors look, and the overall feel or "ethos" of the movie.

The same is true of Christian college kids. My wife and I were on a road trip recently, and we stopped for lunch at a fast-food place in Louisville, Kentucky. In the same fast-food place was the crew team from Wheaton College. Now, the mere mention of the words *crew team* and *Wheaton College* brings to mind a certain upscale, Kennedys-playing-touch-football sort of health, vigor, prosperity, and vitality. The thing is, you know you're around Christian college kids as soon as you walk into a coffee shop in Wheaton, or Ivanhoes in Upland, Indiana. They have a "look" that has something to do with fresh WASPy faces, nice fleece jackets, modesty, and a myriad of other things that I can't quite articulate. But you know it when you see it.

All of this to say I'm acutely aware of the level of cheesiness foisted upon society by Christians over the years, and how hard it is to be associated with that sometimes.

I just watched a film called *The Savages* (with Laura Linney and Phil Seymour Hoffman), which is a depressing emotional beating in the vein of *Running with Scissors*, *The Squid and the Whale*, and to a lesser extent, *Little Miss Sunshine*. It's the Laura Linney Film, which is now, I've discovered, its own genre. That's not to say it's bad; it's just its own depressing, unresolved thing that's more like watching a random neighbor's slightly more stylized life than watching a movie. It's a "thing" just like a Quentin Tarantino film is a thing. Hoffman and Linney, though, were amazing.

The reason I mention this film, now, in this book, is that the Laura Linney Film is often a very accurate and sad representation of what life looks like for American intellectuals without Christ and without the church. The films all follow a similar story arc, which is that hard things happen to intellectuals (a divorce in *Squid*, or a parent dying in *Savages*), those intellectuals have their lives turned upside down by that event, and in the end they get on with their lives, but we don't know for sure if they've learned anything or grown in any significant way.[9] The films always make me sad, though it should be said that I love the performances, and they always make me thankful for pastors and my church body, imperfect though it is. In a way that might very well be cowardly, I know that my church will be there for me when I have to go through awful life events, and it's a comfort.

There are the obvious differences, the first being that everybody in a Linney film is usually either a playwright or a PhD in English. The other difference is that in addition to being tormented by whatever is happening in their lives, all of the characters are almost paralytically introspective, to the point that the entirety of the film feels like an "on crack" version of the object lesson in self-reflexiveness that you learned about in your freshman level communications course. I always end up being thankful that my own friends aren't that introspective, and that I have a rather large Something Else (church) in my life to give attention to, besides myself.

A BLOGOSPHERE DISCUSSION WITH TWO DISGRUNTLED JOHNNIES THAT DIDN'T GO VERY WELL

Another movie—a documentary actually—forms its own sad commentary on how some without Christ look at the church. It also suggests how we should—and should not— present the gospel to an unbeliever. *Christianity Today* called the movie, *Purple State of Mind*, "about as honest a dialogue on the things that both divide and unite us as you will find. With authenticity that doesn't pull punches and intimacy that never loses sight of the big picture, the film recognizes that the conversation, not the conversion, is the commonality."

CT is right in that there is a lot of commonality in the film, in that the two men agree a lot more than they disagree. *Purple State of Mind* ostensibly had something to do with red and blue states, in the political sense, but it was really just a conversation between a really smart, winsome atheist named John Marks and his Christian filmmaker buddy Craig Detweiler who sadly came across as less than courageous, and who Marks shredded throughout most of the film.

The documentary could have easily been titled *Blue State of Mind*. In a blog entry, I charged Detweiler with being "evasive" about his own beliefs, as the atheist grilled him about abortion, gay marriage, and topics of theology. At one point in the film, Marks categorized Detwieler, his former college roommate, as "slippery." And watching the documentary, I concluded in my entry that Detweiler "was a Kleenex. Soft."[10]

Detweiler, a PhD, is an accomplished writer in his own right and the codirector of the Reel Spirituality Institute at Fuller Theological Seminary, and he's a very popular and in-demand speaker on the "Christians who want to make movies" conference circuit. His film, though, makes me wonder if we've lost our audacity[11] as a church. And I'm left wondering how Detweiler squares his performance with 2 Timothy 1:8 (NIV), which reads, "So do not be ashamed to testify about our Lord, or ashamed of me his prisoner."

I got beat up on the *Purple State of Mind* blog by John Marks, the atheist. He rightly called me out on my tone (obnoxious and impulsive—my words), for which I apologized and truly lost a lot of sleep, and then wrongly blamed me (Christians) for civil wars and all manner of other nastiness.[12]

A DISCUSSION *PAS TROIS*

Part of our discussion is reprinted below. It represents an interesting dialogue between a Christian and an atheist who is determined to have the back of his friend who was unwilling to answer any of his questions.

> JOHN: Thanks everyone for your responses. Craig is the missing ingredient here, and I didn't want to respond till he'd had a chance, but given Ted's apology (quite unnecessary), I thought I'd better acknowledge these posts and offer a few thoughts. . . .
>
> First, to Ted, thanks for your words of remorse over the tone of your comment, which, of course, bugged me a little. More significant, however, was the fact that you had bothered to respond with such passion. I felt that it was important to comment in kind and to push Craig to meet the charges in your post head on.
>
> Our documentary and website shouldn't be about the suppression of heated exchange. It should be an encouragement, an emboldening of the impulse, if you will, and every form of discourse should be welcome as long as such discourse leaves room for dialogue. Your post was smart and candid, and I was thrilled to see it.
>
> My rebuke was meant to be a defense of my friend's honor as much as anything else. I wanted Craig to know how I felt about your words, that I thought you'd been unfair in your language, and that you'd missed the subtlety and nuance of Craig's response. A few thousand people around the country have seen this movie now, and we've had plenty of responses in your spirit, but just as many have welcomed Detweiler's "passivity" rapturously, as an antidote, as a sign of change and growth and hope.

I'm not suggesting that he's therefore right just because lots of people like his answers to my questions. I am promoting the idea that you should be more curious about those other responses. . . .

In my humble opinion, Ted responded so vigorously to Craig's positions in the movie because they are not at all passive; they are, in fact, a critique of Ted's position, and a devastating one. . . .

So keep talking. As a non-believer who left behind a religious tradition, I am concerned that our national conversation across the faith line has become trivial at best and destructive at worst. These posts demonstrate signs of life, but they shouldn't stop at an apology for an honest attack.

TED: I commend you for defending the honor of your friend. . . . It's admirable that you and Craig have that kind of friendship, and you were right to do so. And know that you didn't rebuke me into silence, rather, into a humble, thoughtful reflection over what I'd written. . . .

I'll address a couple of your points. I would agree with you in thinking that Craig and I probably have more than a couple of significant doctrinal differences. And I guess when I think of Christians disagreeing my mind doesn't immediately jump to "nastiness," "war," or "Civil War"— terminology you used in your first post. I don't want to think of Craig (or you) in that context.

Also, in researching my last book, *Why We're Not Emergent: By Two Guys Who Should Be* I spent the better part of a year reading and listening to the pro-Detweiler camp as you suggested. Needless to say I disagree, for reasons both doctrinal (more important) and cultural (less important). This discussion speaks to core beliefs about the faith (heaven/hell, authority of Scriptures, knowability of God, etc.) but I don't think the Detweiler position (at least the one he articulated in the film) helps people like you die well. That concerns me. I have unbelieving

WHY WE LOVE THE CHURCH

friends. I want very badly to share eternity with them.

Craig also responded on his blog. He noted how "a Christian's dogmatism" doesn't play well in Hollywood and said a subtler approach is needed. "While esteemed scholars like Al Mohler, Alistair Begg, et. al., have their place offering surety in an era of uncertainty, I am affirming uncertainty in hopes of enticing others to address their doubts to God," he wrote. "The heartfelt questions/confessions/conversations that the film engenders confirms that *Purple State of Mind* speaks to many caught in the old crossfire." For him, "apologetics begins with apologies."

I replied to Craig's blog entry, noting that we disagreed on almost everything. About his film and purpose therein, I wrote, "From where I sat it looked an awful lot like a passionate atheist conversing with a Christian who was trying awfully hard not to offend him. Now, in light of your post, I can see that this is what you were going for and that's fine. It's just a different choice."

My choice is to agree with Paul when it comes to the gospel—to not "be ashamed to testify about our Lord" (2 Tim. 1:8 NIV).

AFTER MY INTERNET THROW-DOWN

I lost sleep over this whole thing, which really was my first real Internet throw-down. The positive by-product of this three-way exchange, besides me seriously considering quitting the blogosphere forever, is the fact that I'm now, sort of, in touch with John Marks. The film whets my appetite for knowing why, exactly, he quit the church and then quit Christianity altogether. I swallow hard and decide to write him despite our, ahem, dubious start.

I realize that it's impossible to really get a feel for why groups of people are put off by the church. I'm excited to dialogue with Marks about it, as he is a somewhat public figure with a track record for communicating well. He is a novelist, journalist, and a former *60 Minutes* producer. His first novel, *The Wall*, was named a *New York Times* Notable Book in 1998. His second, *War Torn*, made *Publishers Weekly*'s Best of 2003. He also just wrote a book that his Web site describes as "a portrait of American Christianity," called *Reasons to Believe.*

It strikes me that for an atheist, Marks has probably done more thinking about the church and churches than a good 95 percent of Christians. And though he doesn't go to church anymore except "once in a while with family and friends," he has clear thoughts on what he sees in them. "As an observer I try to find the authenticity in each church, wherever it lies, whether it repels or attracts me. To me, churches are as individual as people," he told me, "and the dogma is never the same from place to place, changing profoundly with each stylistic alteration, with the felt needs of a particular population, with the access to funds. I don't really look for anything. I wait to see what the church wants to show to me."

What Marks says rings true, especially the part about access to funds and felt needs. One can almost tell what he's going to hear in a church simply by noting its location (inner city, suburbs) and building (style, access to funding). Unfortunately, a church wanting to show Marks anything other than the gospel is going to ring hollow and inauthentic. Even if that "anything" is a big dose of "we love you and will look the other way with regard to the sin in your life."

"Church just never made the case for its relevance in my life," Marks says. "It seemed a social gathering, and I can certainly respect that, but I didn't need it to perform that function in my life, and it offered little else. I don't like to network at parties, for the same reason, but parties offer other pleasures."

Marks articulates his own personal belief system well in another blog post: "I don't have a message of my own to spread. I take pieces of things that seem to make sense and place them next to other pieces that seem to make sense. I do rely on laws and principles that were at one time based in absolute principles of justice, it's true, and perhaps that makes me a hypocrite. At the very least, I am inconsistent."

As Christians I think we do the same things, but with different pieces. The pieces, for me, are my own total depravity (easily understood), and the idea that a real Christ died on a real cross and then really rose three days later to absolve me of that sin and depravity. My other pieces are a loving church, Christian friends who hold me up in prayer, my loving and faithful (to God and each other) parents, and lots of other "proofs" of God's work, including tangible answers to prayer, feelings, and the sense of His presence when I read the Word or have the Word read to me.[13] Perhaps the final, most important piece is election, or the fact that God, in His sovereignty, chose to call me to Himself. And perhaps that's what isn't there or won't be there for Marks, though I couldn't say for sure.

"I haven't been to church for decades for the sake of the experience, except to go with my mother or friends from time to time. I just don't like the contemporary church as a place for reflection, meditation, spirituality," he writes. "They don't seem to have much to do with those things. Also, I don't seek those things in community, I suppose. I do appreciate church as staged drama, as a reenactment of an ancient Mediterranean myth with all kinds of modern variables and augmentations. It's the closest I will ever get to understanding the mind-set of a first-century-AD subject of the Roman Empire; that's how I think of it, a distant echo, a sort of living history, and that's thrilling."

AN ATHEIST ON COMMUNITY

A blog "conversation" is, of course, one-way communication at the time. But there are opportunities to form relationships. Thinking about John Marks, I'm reminded about the believer's call to be faithful to God and not being a direct offense—though the gospel itself may, at times, offend (1 Pet. 2:7–8). We must be gracious and compelling, yet bold and always true to God's declaration of love and judgment.

Finally, I ask Marks if there is anything about the church that he either enjoys or appreciates.

"I do get what the church provides by way of community for people in suburban and exurban America," he writes. "Many of the bigger churches, which come in for so much criticism, are places where people from many different creeds, races and economic classes can gather and feel at home. That has huge value, and it's what most impressed me, the heart of the success. How many other American institutions can claim the same success in integration, if only sporadically?"

Aside from the insinuation that America's urban dwellers have somehow evolved past church,[14] Marks has a point. However, in response to his question of how many other American institutions can claim the same level of integration, in which different races, creeds, and economic classes gather shoulder-to-shoulder, I would add to the list boxing matches (Ever been to a big fight in Vegas? It's a melting pot.), NFL stadiums, NBA arenas, and shopping malls.

All of which is to say that there is more happening in churches than just people coming together for "community."

NOTES

1. *Fireproof is* from the studio responsible for *Facing the Giants* I took a surprising amount of flack on my blog for ripping *Facing the Giants*, a movie that I thought, and still think, was famously bad, even by famously-bad Christian movie standards. I think this not because it wasn't a great effort on the part of some earnest, good-hearted actors and writers (it was); rather, because it really encouraged a sort of prosperity-centered "God as cosmic vending machine" theology, where one begins to pray, and then in the case of Coach, one receives a state championship team, a new truck, and a fetus. This just isn't, in my experience or under-standing of Scripture, how God works most of the time. Which raises the greater question: Are we required to "like" or "support" something like this just because it's "Christian"?

2. I know this language sounds "modern" and antiquated, but it still matters.

3. It's cool now, in some of these books, to bash seminary, and decry how seminary only teaches a person to feel coldly academic toward the Bible. While I'm sure this is true in some cases, it doesn't seem to be the case with the majority of the men I met at the Moody Pastors Confer-ence. And while seminary attendance doesn't ensure biblical knowledge or a healthy church, partly because not all seminaries are good, it certainly can't hurt to go and immerse yourself in Scripture, Greek, Hebrew and preaching instruction for a period of time.

4. Freak out now, if you're uncomfortable with battle metaphors. However, these are used by lots of authors I really respect, including John Piper, J. C. Ryle, and the apostle Paul.

5. Or careless Disgruntled Johnny praying in the woods or meeting with a friend occasionally at Starbucks.

6. Or careless reformed theology snob. I have to admit this hit close to home for me.

7. J. C. Ryle, *Holiness* (Peabody, Mass.: Hendrickson, 2007), 299.

8. I attended one myself, so I had a few years to really hone this theory.

9. At the end of *The Savages* the Linney character adopts a wounded dog that she nurses back to health, this is supposed to be evidence of great personal growth.

10. To read the entire blog posting, go to Ted Kluck, "Brief Comments on the film 'Purple State of Mind,'" June 22, 2008 at www.tedkluck.com/blog1/?m=200806.

11. See also: courage, boldness, relevance.

12. I'm talking here, of course, about the Crusades, which is what I think John was talking about too, in so many words. Kevin does a great job of writing about that later in this text. In short, it doesn't take a whole lot of courage to "apologize" for something your boneheaded forefathers did many years before, though that seems to be the cool thing today nowadays.

13. To wit: Anytime anybody (usually my mother) reads Scripture to me aloud, be it in person or on the telephone, I cry. And I'm not really a cryer. Now, I know this isn't to say, "Hey, Kluck the boxing writer cries every time his mom reads him Scripture so God is real." But still, it's proof to me that there is something special and different about the Word. Or it might be proof to you that I'm a wus.

14. See again: A latent or not-so-latent disrespect for middle America.

Elect from every nation,

Yet one o'er all the earth,

Her charter of salvation,

One Lord, one faith, one birth;

One holy Name she blesses,

Partakes one holy food,

And to one hope she presses,

With every grace endued.

– "The Church's One Foundation," verse 2

CHAPTER **5**

ONE HOLY CATHOLIC CHURCH

C. S. Lewis is famous for many things, among them coining the phrase "chronological snobbery." The phrase refers to the all-too-common tendency among Christians to quickly discount what is old and automatically embrace what is new. We tend to think our problems are original to us and our solutions are one of a kind. We are faddish trend-watchers—ignorant of our own history, obnoxiously dismissive of the practices of our spiritual fathers and mothers, and easily duped.

Although there's much talk these days about our lack of Christian community and the need we have to do our exegesis in the community of faith, the one community we seldom look to for wisdom is the community of the dead. Being inclusive toward the communion of the saints—who represent different centuries, different cultures, and different contexts—seems to be the one type of diversity that doesn't count.

THE WAY WE WEREN'T

Ironically, a cavalier attitude toward Christian history is sometimes most pronounced in those who profess to be the most interested in history. A case in point is the hot-selling book *Pagan Christianity* by Frank Viola and George Barna. The first sentence tells where the book is heading: "Not long after I left the institutional church to begin gathering with Christians in New Testament fashion, I sought to understand how the Christian church ended up in its present state."[1] According to Viola (the book's main author[2]), on one side we have the institutional church—church as we know it—replete with its buildings, paid clergy, sermons, liturgy, and Sunday school classes. On the other side—a long ways away, untainted by pagan influence, Constantine, and the evils of the Catholic Church and the Reformation—we have New Testament Christianity. In three hundred pages and a bazillion footnotes,[3] Viola sets out to explain how the pure, uncorrupted first-century church came to take on its present "institutional form" which "has neither a biblical nor a historical right to function as it does."[4]

Historical Hubris

Pagan Christianity, like most restorationist literature, is full of historical hubris. Granted, traditionalists have their own pride—pride in traditions, order, and a dozen other things, I'm sure. But it is an all-too-common source of pride among strands of evangelicals to think that they are going to be the first ones to be free from all the stains of history and to get right back to the first century.[5] Bob Kauflin, who is quite open to unplanned expressions in worship, writes:

> For years I thought of religious traditions as a hindrance to biblical spirituality. I associated repeated prayers, reciting creeds together, public confession of sin, Scripture readings, church calendars, and

orders of service with legalism and bondage.

I was on a mission to start from scratch in my thinking about corporate worship. I would look only to Scripture rather than depending on anything people had done in previous centuries. I thought I was being original.

Actually, I was simply being ignorant—and proud.[6]

I don't doubt that Viola and others with his bent toward free-flowing worship love the Lord and want people to worship Him in Spirit and truth, but it takes a lot of misplaced guts to demean all of contemporary Christianity, with the exception of the house-church movement Viola belongs to, as "guilty of the error of the Pharisees" and suppressing "the living, breathing, functioning headship of Jesus Christ in His Church."[7] The church is always deserving of some critique, or even a lot of critique at times, but isn't it a bit sweeping to declare that "everything that is done in our contemporary churches has no basis in the Bible"?[8] Yes, the Bible matters more than church history, but at least the Reformers understood that history is not bunk. They took great pains to show that their ideas were not only rooted in Scripture, but were also shared by many, if certainly not all, the church fathers. Viola and Barna have no interest in the catholicity (read: universality) of the church's witness and worship. As they see it, the church has been bankrupt for two thousand years, but with their research, we can finally take the "red pill," have "the curtain pulled back" and see "the true story of where your Christian practices came from."[9]

The arguments in *Pagan Christianity* are grossly overstated. On several occasions as I read Viola's claims I thought, *You would be fine if you stopped right now and made the point that these things [pulpits, stained glass, robes, etc.] don't* have *to be in church, but then you go and try to prove that they* can't. There may be Christians who think church can't exist without pews. For them, Viola's book may be a needed antidote. But just because pews come later in the church's history, or even if pagans used them first, doesn't make them unChristian. If you don't like pews, fine. But they're just benches. Can we not have hinges on our church doors if a nonChristian invented them?[10] This is the same sort of logic I read in conspiracy theorists who claim that we are all worshiping Roman gods because we have church on Sunday (the day of the sun) and prayer meetings on Wednesday (i.e., Woden's Day).

With the "we've finally discovered the truth" tune comes an equally strong "we're modern-day martyrs" vibe. In their book about not wanting to go to church anymore, Wayne Jacobsen and Dave Coleman dedicate the book to "The Blessed Ones—those today and throughout history who [have] been insulted, excluded, and lied about for simply following the Lamb beyond the accepted norms of tradition and culture."[11] Likewise, Viola dedicates *Pagan Christianity* "to our forgotten brothers and sisters throughout the ages who courageously stepped outside the safe bounds of institutional Christianity at the risk of life and limb. You faithfully carried the torch, endured persecution, forfeited reputation, lost family, suffered torture, and spilled your blood to preserve the primitive testimony that Jesus Christ is Head of His Church." Now, I don't doubt Christians get ridiculed at times when they stop going to church, but tortured? Comparing church-leavers to Luther or the Puritans misses the mark, considering Luther was excommunicated and hunted down like a dog and the Puritans were kicked out of the church under the Act of Uniformity.[12] Somehow going to a small-group service doesn't strike me as the same kind of sacrifice. What has become of Christianity when the definition of radical courage and devotion to Christ is that you stop showing up at church? Barna, in a strange piece of logic, suggests that since the church (*ekklesia*) refers to people who are "called out" (*ek kaleo*), Revolutionary Christians shouldn't be afraid to reject the norm, pay the cost, stand apart from the crowd, and honor God by dropping out of Sunday services if that's what He's calling you to do.[13]

So the supposed etymology of the word *church* becomes a rationale for leaving the church. These are strange times indeed.

THE BIG TWO

It would be too tedious to comment on everything Viola thinks is pagan in today's church (and basically it's everything). But I want to comment on two broad areas of his study, because they show up frequently in current anti-church-as-we-know-it literature.

Edifice Complex

The first broad area deals with church buildings. The argument is expressed in several ways: "The church is the people, not the building." Or, "We can't go to church, because we are the church." Or, "You don't need an address to be a church."

The story goes like this. In the beginning, when the church was pure, they met in homes. Christians did not start meeting in their own buildings until the fourth century, under Constantine, "the father of the church building."[14] Then Christians began calling their buildings "churches." Later they called them "temples" and began infusing spiritual significance in the space and architecture, even though there "does not exist a shred of biblical support for the church building."[15] In fact, "it is high time we Christians wake up to the fact that we are being neither biblical nor spiritual by supporting church buildings. . . . If every Christian on the planet would never call a building a church again, this alone would create a revolution in our faith."[16]

Viola makes some valid points. Christians can be obsessed with buildings, wasting lots of time and money on overexpanding facilities. We do sometimes equate a building with the church, when the people are what matter. And the building is not sacred space, at least not in the same way the temple was sacred. I don't think the ground is any holier inside the church than out. So I'm happy for Viola and others to correct mistaken notions some people may have about the importance of church buildings.

But Viola overstates his case. For starters, he makes too much of the fact that early Christians met in homes. They didn't meet in homes in an effort to start the world's first nonreligious religion. As early Christianity scholar Wayne Meeks writes, "The practice of meeting in private houses was probably *an expedient* used by Jews in many places as it was for the Pauline Christians, to judge from the remains of synagogue buildings at Dura-Europos, Stobi, Delos, and elsewhere that were adapted from private dwellings."[17] The Christians met in homes for three hundred years because their faith was illegal. They didn't have anywhere else to meet, which is why buildings started popping up after Constantine decriminalized Christianity. There is no command for Christians to meet in small numbers in homes and no reason to think they did so for any other reasons than necessity and convenience.

> CHRISTIANS MET IN HOMES FOR THREE HUNDRED YEARS BECAUSE THEIR FAITH WAS ILLEGAL. THEY DIDN'T HAVE ANYWHERE ELSE TO MEET.

It's also worth pointing out, as Ben Witherington mentioned in his excellent blog review of *Pagan Christianity*, that a Roman house, especially with the courtyard, could be quite spacious, allowing for up to one hundred people in attendance. So "house church" doesn't necessarily mean small-group Bible study.[18] Moreover, the early Christians did *not* gather exclusively in homes. In Acts we see that they also met in Solomon's Portico (Acts 5:12), still went to synagogues (3:1), and occasionally rented lecture halls, like the hall of Tyrannus in Ephesus (19:9). Archaeological evidence also demonstrates that they sometimes met in caves.[19] Further, excavations have discovered a house from the middle of the third century (before Constantine!) that was extensively remodeled, including an enlarged meeting hall, into a building "entirely devoted to religious functions" after which "all domestic activities ceased.[20]

On top of this we have James 2:2, where James talks of a man who "comes into your *synagogue*," which our English Bibles translate "assembly" but may also refer to an actual synagogue building. Considering that James was writing to Jews (1:1) and that "synagogue" was the common term used for religious buildings among Jews, it is possible that James 2:2 makes reference to some early Jewish Christians meeting in their old religious buildings.

Here's the bottom line: The whole conversation about church buildings is much ado about nothing. You have to meet somewhere. Even if you don't own a building, presumably your worship gathering does not meet in a random, always-changing, undisclosed location (unless you're facing persecution). You do have some address. There is some place where your church meets. Sure, strictly speaking, you may want to think of that place as more of a meeting house (*a la* the Puritans) than a church. But if you call the building "a church" I think God will understand. And if, without getting superstitious, you think *I may worship God everywhere I go, but this is the only place I get to worship Him with the body of Christ, receive the sacraments, and celebrate His resurrection every Lord's Day; let's set this apart in some way*—that's not a bad impulse either. Besides, many church buildings, like ours, get used almost every night of the week. Sure, a building costs money and takes effort to maintain, but Bible studies, bridal showers, Thanksgiving meals, English as a Second Language classes, campus events, and a hundred other things take place in our building all the time precisely because they wouldn't work in someone's home.

Viola is right to quote John Newton when he said, "Let not him who worships under steeple condemn him who worships under a chimney."[21] But should not the reverse also be true? Let not him who worships on couches in the living room condemn him who worships with pews, pulpits, stained glass, and a fellowship hall.

Spirituality and Spontaneity

The second broad area of concern has to do with worship. Viola objects to the traditional order of worship which, he maintains, rarely varies and is essentially the same in all Protestant churches. By contrast, "the meetings of the early church were marked by every-member functioning, spontaneity, freedom, vibrancy, and open participation." Viola never tires of telling us that the traditional order of service we are used to is "unscriptural" and "heavily influenced by paganism."[22] Our formulaic worship services encourage passivity, limit the gifts of the body, and rip out the heart of primitive Christianity which was informal and free of ritual, he argues.[23] Instead of our usual service which "strangles the headship of Jesus Christ" and is "shamefully boring,"[24] we should embrace the "glorious, free-flowing, open-participatory, every-member-functioning church meetings that we see in 1 Corinthians 14:26 and Hebrews 10:24–25."[25]

What are we to make of Viola's assessment of traditional worship and his prescription of truly biblical worship? Let me make several observations.

First, this description of the usual Protestant worship service is grossly uncharitable. It would be one thing to argue for another option, but Viola insists that the worship in most of our churches is not simply lacking in some ways, but thoroughly unbiblical, pagan, and dreadfully dull. Are we really to believe that true biblical worship has been in hiatus for about two millennia and is just now getting a second chance with charismatic house-church meetings?

And why do traditional church services always have to be described with the most unflattering language possible? In the "church is lame" critique, I've read the usual Protestant worship service described as watching a praise concert and listening to a teaching,[26] two-hour-a-week dumping ground for guilt,[27] on the best days tolerable and on the worst painful,[28] a robotic routine conducted without emotion, passion, or zeal,[29] and little more than sitting in a sanctuary once a week.[30] It's also been called a religious show that takes place on Sunday, and a mindless observation of meaningless routines.[31] So much for the benefit of the doubt. Why can't we describe our worship as "justified sinners coming to receive more grace" or "God's people gathering with all their imperfections to worship the risen Christ" or "the company of the redeemed joining voice in song and exulting in the preached word"?

Second, we must keep in mind that the description of worship in 1 Corinthians 14 is not the only information we have on worship in the New Testament. We know, for example, from Acts that the first Christians devoted themselves to the apostles' teaching in their gatherings (2:42) and their services could involve long preaching (20:9). The services at Corinth are not meant to provide a normative blueprint for Christian worship. In fact, the reason we are given such detail about the gatherings in Corinth is because they were *too* free-flowing. First Corinthians 14 is Paul's attempt to lay down some order for the church, not an exhortation to more spontaneity (14:40). Paul is concerned that the women not overstep their bounds (14:34), tongues be interpreted (14:5ff.), and the speakers be limited to two or three (14:27, 29).

Agreed, churches should provide informal times of sharing, whether that takes place in a Sunday service or in small groups or in Sunday school classes or all of the above. But to suggest that the New Testament mandates nothing but spontaneous, free-flowing sharing/testimony services goes against the reason for 1 Corinthians 14 and the fuller scope of the New Testament.

Third, Jesus is not the head worship leader of the service as Viola argues (without evidence) numerous times. Jesus is the object of our worship, and Jesus ministers to us in worship. But the New Testament never suggests that Christ leads our services.[32] True, the *Spirit* ought to infuse our services, and He may even move us to do something previously unplanned. Maybe that's what Viola has in mind.

WE SHOULDN'T THINK SPONTANEITY EQUALS SPIRITUALITY.

But even here, we shouldn't think spontaneity equals spirituality. Why is a service considered more "Spirit-led" if the Spirit puts the service together on Sunday morning instead of Tuesday afternoon? Deviating from the script on Sunday is fine and at times clearly called for, but let's not forget that there's nothing wrong with calling on the Spirit to help us put together the script in the first place.

Fourth, many house-church proponents assume rather simplistically that informality is good and formality is bad. Of course, there are stilted liturgical services full of rote formality and dead traditionalism. But can nothing good come out of a well-structured, liturgical, more high-church service? In fact, one of the main critiques of evangelical worship, and the main reason people jump ship for Canterbury, Rome, or Greece, is because our worship lacks any kind of otherness. It's too much aw-shucks and "Good morning everybody" with little to suggest that what we are gathered to do on Sunday morning is awe inspiring and set apart.

True, Romans 12 teaches that all of life is worship. But the underlying assumption behind texts like 1 Corinthians 14 is that there is also something unique about the saints gathered for corporate worship. Tongues were good in one setting, but used the same way they were not appropriate for the gathered assembly. There are different "rules" that apply—namely, the rule of edification.

Or to look at it from another angle, what we do on Sunday is a foretaste of the ceaseless worship that will be ours in heaven and a reflection of the glorious worship taking place presently around the throne. These occasions of heavenly worship, in texts like Isaiah 6 and Revelation 4, hardly smack of casual, free-flowing informality. An informal service in a living room can be pleasing to God; and so can a structured service with responsive readings, set prayers, and expositional preaching under a vaulted ceiling. Pagan worship for Paul had everything to do with idols, false gods, and demons, and nothing to do with buildings, clergy, and orders of worship.[33]

The informal house-church service itself cannot always escape the clutches of boredom and predictability. In the Viola model of the house church, one person shares a word from the Lord, then someone makes up a song on the spot and others join in, then someone else prays, then another person shares what she learned from the Lord that week, then another person reads a poem or tells a story, and so forth. The whole experience is supposed to be full of "spontaneity, creativity, and freshness."[34] But haven't we all been in informal group settings where the same person talks week after week—and usually not very well? Haven't we all been made to sit through sharing times where some dear soul can't seem to land the testimony plane? How long will people put up with bad poetry in the name of creativity?

Again, I'm thankful for these more casual times, and churches should provide for them in some way. I'm blessed whenever we have our unstructured times for congregational sharing. But won't the people attending the glorious free-for-all service every week get tired of shallow spur-of-the-moment songs that won't be around in ten minutes, let alone ten centuries? Won't some of them start hoping for more regular sharing from brother Joe who is obviously a gifted teacher and less from brother Jim who, bless his heart, gets his ideas from trolling the blogosphere? Won't people eventually get bored listening to the umpteenth prayer request for Aunt Bertha's gout? Every house group will fall into a liturgy—some will plan for it and others won't.

I'll say it one more time: there's nothing wrong—and much good, in fact—with these kind of informal meetings . . . in the proper context. But I doubt that over a lifetime they will prove to be, for most folks, as scintillating and fresh as they seem the first several times around.

Finally, Viola's reconstruction of the early church is hugely mistaken. The worship of the early church was simply not without ritual and structure.

This final point is really important. Think of what we find in the New Testament: a holy meal celebrated frequently (Lord's Supper); an initiatory rite signifying those who belong to the Christian community (baptism); a day set apart (the "Lord's Day" mentioned by John in Rev. 1:10, probably alluded to by Luke in Acts 20:7, and referenced by Pliny and Justin Martyr); the singing of psalms, hymns, and spiritual songs (Eph. 5:18–20); the probable recitation of other hymns or confessional poems (Phil 2:6–11; Col. 1:15–20; 1 Tim. 3:16); the teaching and reading of Old Testament Scripture (1 Tim. 4:13); contemporary epistles commanded to be read in the churches (1 Thess. 5:27). Add to this list numerous doxologies (e.g., Gal. 1:5) and benedictions (e.g., Gal. 6:18), liturgical "amens" (1 Cor. 14:16), holy kisses (Rom. 16:16), and the "maranatha" (quite possibly a set prayer for after Communion [1 Cor. 11:26; 16:22]), and even future liturgical formulas to be repeated and sung by the saints and angels in heaven (see examples in

Revelation chapters 4–5, 7, 11, 15–16, 19, 22). We see evidence of patterns and structure all over the place.

Moreover, an examination of early church documents like Clement's *Epistle to the Corinthians* (c. 95), Ignatius' *Epistle to the Smyrnaeans* (c. 112), *The Didache* (early second century), *The First Apology of Justin Martyr* (c. 155), and *The Apostolic Traditions of Hippolytus* (c. 200) show the existence of specific worship orders in the early church, including responsive readings, Communion instructions, liturgical responses, prayer formulas, blessing formulas, and various rules for teachers and preachers.[35] Our worship does not need to be identical to that of the early church, especially when we move outside the New Testament to the testimony of the church fathers, but to argue for a completely spontaneous, structureless, antiliturgical, brand-new-every-week worship service in the first centuries of the church is an argument against the plain facts of history.

ONE HELLISH CATHOLIC CHURCH?

This chapter is about history—about the historical reasons Christians and nonChristians offer for their disenchantment with the church. To this point we've talked about how some Christians claim we have strayed from our own earlier, more pristine history. Yet everyone knows that parts of our history were not pristine. During those embarrassing and sometimes hideous moments, the church of Jesus Christ has not acted anything like Jesus Christ. And there have been plenty of those moments over the last two thousand years. We cannot ignore the sleazy televangelists, crooked pastors, heinous popes, and hypocritical churchgoers. Nor can we dismiss the unnecessary bloodshed and backward thinking in our history. But history is seldom simple. And sometimes our understanding of it is just plain incorrect.

Ever since Donald Miller's *Blue Like Jazz*, it has become popular for

Christians to apologize to anyone who will listen for all the ways the church has screwed up. In one of the more memorable stories from the book, Miller tells of the time he set up a confessional booth on his very liberal, anti-Christian campus. People wandered in thinking they were supposed to confess their sins, but instead Miller and his friends confessed the sins of the church, apologizing for the Crusades, televangelists, for neglecting the poor and lonely, and misrepresenting Jesus on their campus.[36] I've also read Christians confess our complicity in the Spanish Inquisition, the Salem witch trials, and bombing abortion clinics.[37] More recently, I read of a pastor who did a five-week series on "Confessions of a Sinful Church" where he apologized for "our self-righteousness and hypocrisy," "our endorsement of slavery," "our mistreatment of homosexuals," "the medieval crusades," and "saying the earth is flat."[38] I like the creativity of the approach. I like the idea of being honest about our mistakes. But there are some real dangers in confessing the sins of the church.

Truth about a Flat Earth

The biggest dangers in confessing our ecclesiastical sins is that we don't get our own story straight. For example, the church did not object to Columbus' voyage because it thought the earth was flat. That's a myth that has been erroneously believed since Andrew Dickson White, the founder and first president of Cornell University, authored his influential study, "A History of the Warfare of Science with Theology in Christendom" in 1896. The "sundry wise men of Spain" who challenged Columbus did not do so on account of their belief in the earth's flatness, but because they thought Columbus had underestimated the circumference of the earth, which he had.[39] Every educated person in Columbus's day knew the earth was round.

Jeffrey Burton Russel argues that during the first fifteen centuries of the

Christian era "nearly unanimous scholarly opinion pronounced the earth spherical, and by the fifteenth century all doubt had disappeared."[40] *Sphere* by the title of the most popular medieval textbook on astronomy which was written in the thirteenth century, and generations before Columbus's voyage, Cardinal Pierre d'Ailly, chancellor of the University of Paris, wrote, "Although there are mountains and valleys on the earth, for which it is not perfectly round, it approximates very nearly to roundness."[41] Centuries earlier, the Venerable Bede (673–735) taught that the world was round, as did Bishop Virgilius of Salzburg (eighth century), Hildegard of Bingen (twelfth century) and Thomas Aquinas (thirteenth century), all four of whom are canonized saints.

Truth about the Slave Trade

And while it's true, shamefully true, that American Christians in the South defended chattel slavery, we need to put this sad fact in context. By the nineteenth century, slavery had existed for a long time, and it was usually not an ethnic or racial thing. Africans had more slaves of their own than were sent to the New World. Muslim slave trading began centuries before Europeans discovered the New World and it continued longer, being legally abolished in Saudi Arabia in 1962.

Of course, this doesn't mean Christians have no complicity in the evils of slavery, but we should remember that slavery was eradicated chiefly due to Christians and Christian nations. The overthrow of slavery (after near-universal slavery for almost of all of recorded human history) came about from two main factors: the rise of nation states (so it became too dangerous to go raid other peoples) and Christian opposition to its practice.

For all its grave faults, European imperialism is largely responsible for ending slavery. Starting in the nineteenth century, the British stamped out slavery in their Empire, which at that time covered a fourth of the world. They destroyed slave trading ships, made slavery illegal, and blockaded islands and coasts until slavery was shut down. Thomas Sowell, the African-American economist writes, "It would be hard to think of any other crusade pursued so relentlessly for so long by any nation, at such mounting costs, without any economic or other tangible benefit to itself."[42] And the crusade was championed by Christians, William Wilberforce chief among them.

Furthermore, it's not as if nineteenth-century Christians were the first ones to object to slavery. Christians didn't begin seeing slavery as being

CHRISTIANS DIDN'T BEGIN SEEING SLAVERY AS BEING WRONG STARTING IN THE NINETEENTH CENTURY.

wrong starting in the nineteenth century. As early as the seventh century, Saint Bathilde (wife of King Clovis II) became famous for her campaign to stop slave trading and free all the slaves in the kingdom. In 851 Saint Anskar began his efforts to halt the Viking slave trade.

In the thirteenth century, Thomas Aquinas argued that slavery was a sin, and a series of popes upheld the position. During the 1430s the Spanish colonized the Canary Islands and began to enslave the native population. Pope Eugene IV issued a bull, giving everyone fifteen days from receipt of his bull, "to restore to their earlier liberty all and each person of either sex who were once residents of said Canary Islands . . . These people are to be totally and perpetually free and are to be let go without exaction or reception of any money."[43] The bull didn't help much, but that is owing to the weakness of the church's power at the time, not indifference to slavery. Pope Paul III made a similar pronouncement in 1537. Slavery was condemned in papal bulls in 1462, 1537, 1639, 1741, 1815, and 1839. In America, the first abolitionist tract was published in 1700 by Samuel Sewall, a devout Puritan. Meanwhile, Enlightenment bigwigs like Hobbes, Locke, Voltaire, Montesquieu, and Burke all supported slavery. I am not trying to rewrite history here and make the record of the church into one long string of unbroken heroism. But since we get the impression from so many folks, Christians and nonChristians alike, that the church has been an unmitigated disaster on social issues since the beginning of time, we should take the time to get the rest of the story, in context and unsensationalized.

Those Abominable Crusades

Let me mention just one more example because it is brought up so often and with so little understanding of the actual facts. I am speaking, of course, about the Crusades.

The Crusades refer to a series of military expeditions over several centuries, beginning with the First Crusade in 1096 through the end of the Fifth Crusade in 1221, and continuing on in more sporadic fashion up until the Reformation. The term *Crusade* is not a medieval word. It is a modern word. It comes from *crucesignati* ("those signed by the cross"), a term used occasionally after the twelfth century to refer to what we now call "crusaders."[44] Contrary to popular opinion, the Crusades did not begin as a holy war whose mission was to convert the heathen by the sword. In fact, very few of the crusaders saw their mission as an evangelistic one. The initial purpose of the Crusades, and the main military goal throughout the Middle Ages, was quite simply to reclaim Christian lands captured by Muslim armies.

The popular conception of ignorant, cruel, and superstitious crusaders attacking peaceful, sophisticated Muslims comes largely from Sir Walter Scott's novel, *The Talisman* (1825) and Sir Steven Runciman's three-volume *History of the Crusades* (1951–54), the latter of which concludes with the famous summation now shared by most everyone: "the Holy War itself was nothing more than a long act of intolerance in the name of God, which is the sin against the Holy Ghost."[45]

Scott and Runciman did much to shape the popular and entirely negative view of the Crusades, but it isn't as if they had no material to work with. The Crusades were often barbaric and often produced spectacular failures—all in the name of Jesus. Children died needlessly. Coalitions splintered endlessly. Jews were sometimes persecuted mercilessly. Ancient cities were ransacked foolishly. And on occasion (e.g., the Wendish Crusade) infidels were forced to convert or die, while the crusaders holding the swords were guaranteed immortality. In short, many of the Christians who went to war under the sign of the cross conducted themselves as if they knew nothing of the Christ of the cross.

But that's not the whole story. The Crusades is also the story of thousands of godly men, women, and children who sacrificed time, money, and health to reclaim holy lands in distant countries overrun by Muslims. The

THE CRUSADERS COULD BE SAVAGE, BUT THEY COULD ALSO BE PIOUS, COMPASSIONATE, AND COURAGEOUS.

Christians of the East had suffered mightily at the hands of the Turks and Arabs. It was only right, it seemed to medieval Christians, to go and help their fellow Christians and reclaim their land and property.

Many crusaders were knights who, with their families, left lands and titles. They saw their journey to the Middle East as an act of piety, a pilgrimage to Jerusalem, the center of the earth and the center of their spiritual world. To be sure, the crusaders could be arrogant and savage, but they could also be pious, compassionate (e.g., the Hospitallers), and courageous.

And they did not always fail. The First Crusade, unlike most of the others, actually worked. Against all odds, a fractious group of Christians made their way from Western Europe to the Middle East and conquered two of the best-defended cities in the world (Antioch and Jerusalem). Their triumph was nothing short of remarkable, and for the crusaders, it signaled nothing less than the hand of God restoring His city to His people.

A popular poem of the fifteenth century captured the heartbeat of the crusading spirit:

> Our faith was strong in th' Orient/ It ruled in all of Asia/ In Moorish lands and Africa/ But now for us these lands are gone/ 'Twould even grieve the hardest stone. . . . We perish sleeping one and all/ The wolf has come into the stall/ And steals the Holy Church's sheep/ The while the shepherd lies asleep/ Four sisters of our Church you find/ They're of the patriarchic kind/ Constantinople, Alexandria/ Jerusalem, Antiochia/ But they've been forfeited and sacked/ And soon the head will be attacked.[46]

We are right to deplore the cruelty meted out by crusading Christians, but we should not ignore their plight. Christian lands had been captured. Surely, they thought, this could not stand. For an American, it's as if Al-Qaeda sacked Washington D.C., set up shop for bin Laden in the White House, and turned the Lincoln Memorial into a terrorist training center. It would be unthinkable, not to mention cowardly, for no one to storm the city, liberate its captives, and reclaim our nation's capital. We should never excuse the atrocities that occurred under the banner of the cross during the Crusades, but we should, at least, take pause to understand why they set out on what seems to us to be a fool's errand.

We should also resist the temptation to blame present-day Muslim extremism on the Crusades. This is not to say that the Crusades don't loom large in the Islamic consciousness. It is to say that this was not always the case. The Crusades were always a big deal in the Christian West, but for Muslims, as late as the seventeenth century, it was just another futile attempt by the infidels to halt the inevitable expansion of Islam. From the time of the prophet Muhammad through the Reformation, Muslims conquered three-fourths of Christian lands. Once the Muslims united under Saladin, the crusaders, themselves divided, were no match for the armies of Islam.

The Crusades were not a major factor in shaping the Islamic world. The term for the Crusades, *harb-al-salib*, was only introduced in the Arab language in the mid-nineteenth century, and the first Arabic history of the Crusades was not written until 1899. Because the Crusades were unsuccessful, they simply did not matter much to Muslims. But all this began to change when European nations colonized Muslim nations and brought their schools and textbooks which hailed the gallant crusaders and heroic knights who tried to bring Christianity and civilization to the Middle East. Like sports, like war, like life—when you're winning, you don't care who's losing; but when you're losing, it matters a lot who's beating you.

Though we should not be fans of the Crusades, we must be careful in our denunciation of them and other parts of the church's history we deem to be criminal. Today, we fight for nation-states and democracy. Back then, they fought for religion and holy lands. Their reasons for war seem wrong to us, but no more than our reasons would seem wrong to them. Thomas Madden writes:

> It is easy enough for modern people to dismiss the crusades as morally repugnant and cynically evil. Such judgments, however, tell us more about the observer than the observed. They are based on uniquely modern (and, therefore, Western) values. If, from the safety of our modern world, we are quick to condemn the medieval crusader, we should be mindful that he would be just as quick to condemn us. Our infinitely more destructive wars waged for the sake of political and social ideologies would, in his opinion, be lam-

entable wastes of human life. In both societies, the medieval and the modern, people fight for what is most dear to them. That is fact of human nature that is not so changeable.[47]

A SORRY BUNCH OF CHRISTIANS

If getting the story wrong, or at least less nuanced than it should be, is the biggest danger with confessing the church's sins, the other big danger is that we are not really confessing any of our own mistakes. Back in 1940, C. S. Lewis penned a striking article for *The Guardian* entitled "Dangers of National Repentance." His basic point is that it is always dangerous when we are apologizing for something we disdain in someone else. Some solidarity with your country or your own history can be a good thing, but it can also easily turn into the sin of pride where we "confess" all the stupid things our benighted forefathers weren't smart enough to avoid. "The first and fatal charm of national repentance is, therefore, the encouragement it gives us to turn from the bitter task of repenting of our own sins to the congenial one of bewailing—but, first, of denouncing—the conduct of others."[48]

More recently, physician and essayist Theodore Dalrymple has labeled this phenomenon the "False Apology Syndrome." The syndrome is dangerous because it allows us to feel good without having to be good. We get all of the moral high ground that comes with confession and none of the personal pain. "The habit of public apology for things for which one bears no personal responsibility changes the whole concept of a virtuous person, from one who exercises the discipline of virtue to one who expresses correct sentiment. The most virtuous person of all is he who expresses it loudest and to most people . . . The end result is likely to be self-satisfaction and ruthlessness accompanied by unctuous moralizing, rather than a determination to behave well."[49] We get to feel grandiose for "our" guilt without actually

WHY WE LOVE THE CHURCH

having to change.

It would not be an example of real humility for me to stand on my soapbox and confess America's high divorce rate, our alarming number of out-of-wedlock births, and the countless abortions we perform. Perhaps some Americans would disagree with me that these are actual sins (which is more than can be said for confessing the Crusades or slavery), but it still isn't much of a confession on my part. Nor would it be big of me to preach a series of sermons apologizing for the church's faults where I lament our wicked popes, our positive-thinking Jesus, and our watered-down seeker-friendly megaplexes. I already think all of those are wrong and I always have. And I had no part in them. Such a sermon series would be viewed as thinly disguised disdain for other people's problems. Depending on the context, it may take courage to denounce certain societal ills and those in power may need to be rebuked for their complicity in perpetrating evil, but then I should just argue against these evils and not claim the moral high ground by attempting to apologize for them, especially when I am confessing the sins of different people in a different place at a different time in history.

Now, if at one time I had championed these things, then maybe my confession would be worth something. "When a man over forty tries to repent the sins of England and to love her enemies," writes Lewis, "he is attempting something costly; for he was brought up to certain patriotic sentiments which cannot be mortified without a struggle. But an educated man who is now in his twenties usually has no such sentiment to mortify. In art, in literature, in politics, he has been, ever since he can remember, one of an angry and restless minority; he has drunk in almost with his mother's milk a distrust of English statesmen and a contempt for the manners, pleasures, and enthusiasm of his less-educated fellow countrymen."[50]

Younger generations today face these same dangers with regard to the

136

church. In confessing all the sins of the church, we have everything to gain and nothing to mortify. This isn't to suggest that the church hasn't gotten things dreadfully wrong, but it is to suggest that slavery and the Crusades are not the things thirtysomething Americans are likely to get wrong today. We would do well to listen to Lewis from seven decades ago: "The communal sins which they should be told to repent are those of their own age and class—its contempt for the uneducated, its readiness to suspect evil, its self-righteous provocations of public obloquy, its breaches of the Fifth Commandment. Of these sins I have heard nothing among them. Till I do, I must think their candour towards the national enemy a rather inexpensive virtue."[51]

To be fair, some of the confessions I've read, like Miller's, also apologize for personal failings and not just the sins of a faceless church of years gone by. But even here, the apology can be dangerously cheap, more of a clearing the throat than an actual pricked conscience. It's all too easy for me to

> **SAYING "SORRY" FOR THE CHURCH'S SINS, IF IT MUST BE DONE, SHOULD ONLY BE DONE WITH GREAT HEARTACHE.**

say, "I'm sorry for not doing more to help the poor, and I'm sorry I haven't been more loving, and I'm sorry I haven't done more for the homeless." But is this real repentance if I don't go out and do something differently after my confession? Maybe Miller lived differently as a result of his confession. It would be wrong for me to assume he didn't. But before we loudly protest all our general failings, we would do well to remember that repentance entails a change of direction and not merely a public declaration that "I could have done more." We shouldn't say we're sorry because it sounds good or makes us look good before others, but because we actually feel regret for some wrongdoing and are intent on living more like Christ in the future.

Just as crucially, saying "sorry" for the church's sins, if it must be done, should only be done with great heartache. The office of communal repentance, says Lewis, "can be profitably discharged only by those who discharge it with reluctance." A son rebuking his mother may be necessary and even edifying, "but only if we are quite sure that he has been a good son and that, in his rebuke, spiritual zeal is triumphing, not without agony, over strong natural affection. The moment there is reason to suspect that he *enjoys* rebuking her—that he believes himself to be rising above the natural level while he is still, in reality, groveling below it in the unnatural—the spectacle becomes merely disgusting. The hard sayings of our Lord are wholesome to those only who find them hard."[52] While only God knows the heart, I fail to see signs of reluctance from those who write about all the ways the church "sucks." I don't sense that their critiques come from a broken heart, much like conservatives can "confess" the sins of America with a self-righteous swagger. I see little evidence in today's church critics of spiritual zeal rising above strong natural affection.

To the contrary, I see the church derided with mockery and scorn. I see critics exaggerating her weaknesses and incapable of affirming any of her strengths. I see many leaving the church instead of loving her for better or for worse. I see lots of my peers who have 20/20 vision for the church's failings, but are nearsighted to their own pride, self-importance, and mutual self-congratulation. I see a willful ignorance to the church's history, a simplistic understanding of its past errors, and a childish impatience for her current struggles.

To be sure, let us lament with broken hearts the impurities yet to be washed clean in Christ's bride. But let us never forget that the first errors to confess are not those sins belonging to our grandparents or the crusaders, but our own.

NOTES

1. Frank Viola and George Barna, *Pagan Christianity,* rev. ed. (Carol Stream, Ill: Tyndale, 2008), xiii.

2. I'll be referring to Frank Viola as the author because the book is basically a reprint of the same book written by Viola back in 2002. Barna's name, it seems, has been added to give the book a broader appeal. But the text has changed very little.

3. Viola relies heavily on older, secondary sources to substantiate his claims. He is not very conversant with primary sources and ignores important documents like the *Didache*. The multitude of footnotes give an illusion of breathtakingly comprehensive research, but it's much less than meets the eye.

4. Ibid., xviii, xx.

5. Cf. Neil Cole, *Organic Church* (San Francisco: Jossey-Bass, 2005), 48.

6. Bob Kauflin, *Worship Matters:* (Wheaton, Ill.: Crossway, 2008), 189.

7. Viola and Barna, *Pagan Christianity*, xviix, viii.

8. Ibid., 4.

9. Ibid., 7. The image of "the red pill" comes from *The Matrix*. Several recent books, including *The Shack*, *Wide Open Spaces*, and *Organic Church*, liken their discoveries about the institutional church to the "red pill" that opens our eyes to the truth—in this case the truth about church as we now know it.

10. To give one more example, according to Viola steeples defy the reality of the incarnation and indwelling of the Holy Spirit by pointing up, as if God were not with us (33). This is too clever by half. Besides, didn't Jesus ascend into heaven? Isn't Jesus depicted as coming down through the clouds at His second coming? So what's the harm in church architecture pointing up? Have a steeple or not, but we shouldn't read pagan influence into our particular dislikes with the traditional church.

11. Jake Colsen, *So You Don't Want to Go to Church Anymore* (Los Angeles: Windblown, 2006), front matter. Jake Colsen is the pseudonym for the Jacobsen-Coleman writing team.

12. For an unfortunate example of this sort of comparison, see Sarah Cunningham, *Dear Church* (Grand Rapids: Zondervan, 2006), 27–28.

13. George Barna, *Revolution:* (Carol Stream, Ill: Tyndale, 2005), 113–14.

14. Viola and Barna, *Pagan Christianity*, 21.

15. Ibid., 42.

16. Ibid., 43

17. Wayne A. Meeks, *The First Urban Christians* (New Haven: Yale Univ. Press, 1983), 80. Emphasis is mine.

18. This point was made by the New Testament scholar Ben Witherington on his blog benwitherington.blogspot.com. On July 2, 2008 I accessed the first two parts (posted June 30 and July 1) of his extremely helpful review of *Pagan Christianity*. Hereafter, I will cite the this material as "Witherington Blog Review."

19. Witherington Blog Review.

20. Michael L. White, *Building God's House in the Roman World: Architectural Adaption Among Pagans, Jews, and Christians* (Baltimore: Johns Hopkins Univ. Press, 1990), 120; as quoted in Rodney Stark, *The Rise of Christianity* (San Francisco: Harper Collins, 1996), 6.

21. Viola and Barna, *Pagan Christianity*, 43.

22. Ibid., 48, 50, 75.

23. Ibid., 77.

24. Ibid., 76.

25. Ibid., 55.

26. Wayne Jacobsen, Appendix, in Jake Colsen, *So You Don't Want to Go to Church Anymore: An Unexpected Journey* (Los Angeles: Windblown Media, 2006), 182.

27. Ibid., 187.

28. Brian Sanders, *Life After Church: God's Call to Disillusioned Christians* (Downers Grove, IL: InterVarsity Press, 2007), 13.

29. "Joann" in Sanders, *Life After Church*, 40.

30. Sarah Cunningham, *Dear Church: Letters From a Disillusioned Generation* (Grand Rapids: Zondervan, 2006), 25.

31. Neil Cole, *Organic Church* (San Francisco: Jossey-Bass, 2005), xxv; and Barna, *Revolution*, 14.

32. See Witherington Blog Review.

33. Again, many of these insights are drawn from Witherington's helpful online review.

34. Viola and Barna, *Pagan Christianity*, 78.

35. See J. B. Lightfoot, *The Apostolic Fathers* (Grand Rapids: Baker, 1976); *Liturgies of the Western Church*, Bard Thompson, comp. (New York: Meridian Books, 1961); *Documents of the Christian Church,* 2nd ed., Henry Bettenson, comp. and ed. (London: Oxford Univ. Press, 1963).

36. Donald Miller, *Blue like Jazz* (Nashville, Nelson, 2003), 118.

37. Steve Conrad, "I'm Sorry" in Spencer Burke, *Out of the Ooze* (Colorado Springs, NavPress, 2007), 22.

38. The example comes from David Kinnaman and Gabe Lyons, *UnChristian* (Grand Rapids: Baker, 2007), 55–56.

39. Rodney Stark, *For the Glory of God: How Monotheism Led to Reformations, Science, Witch-Hunts, and the End of Slavery* (Princeton: Princeton Univ. Press, 2003), 122.

40. Ibid.

41. Ibid.

42. Thomas Sowell, *Black Rednecks and White Liberals* (San Francisco: Encounter Books, 2005), 123.

43. Stark, *For the Glory of God*, 330.

44. Thomas F. Madden, The *New Concise History of the Crusades* (Lanham, Md.: Rowman and Littlefield, 2005), 1.
45. Ibid., 216.
46. Ibid., 204.
47. Ibid., 223.
48. C. S. Lewis, "Dangers of National Repentance" in *God in the Dock*, Walter Hooper, ed. (Grand Rapids: Eerdmans, 1970), 190.
49. Theodore Dalrymple, "False Apology Syndrome—I'm Sorry for Your Sins," from www. incharacter.org, accessed October 14, 2008.
50. Lewis, "Dangers of National Repentance," 190.
51. Ibid., 191.
52. Ibid. (emphasis in original).

These people live in a kind of mist or fog. They see nothing clearly, and do not know what they believe. They have not made up their minds about any great point in the Gospel, and seem content to be honorary members of all schools of thought.

– J. C. Ryle, *Holiness*

As has been said, the church of Jesus Christ would be like Noah's ark; the stench inside would be unbearable if it weren't for the storm outside.

– Charles Colson, *Being the Body*

CHAPTER 6

SNAPSHOTS OF CHURCHED PEOPLE (INCLUDING CHUCK COLSON AND ART MONK)

C huck Colson, seventy-six at the time of this writing, is a member of First Baptist Church in Naples, Florida, and has been for twenty years. He's also famous. For the record he looks forward to the preaching and camaraderie he receives there even though he admits that it's tough for his experience to be "normal" as a celebrity congregant.

Colson is that rare American evangelical celebrity in that he doesn't pastor the church he's in. And he's also rare in that he's sort of become famous twice—once for being Richard Nixon's "hatchet man" and going to prison for indiscretions linked to the Watergate scandal, and later for becoming an influential evangelical author, speaker, and leader. If I had to describe Naples, Florida, in a sentence or so, it would be something like "affluent retirement community." Chuck Colson is probably one of the only congregants at First Baptist who has been to prison. He spent less than a year on the inside, but has been going back for thirty-two years with the ministry he founded, Prison Fellowship.

There are a couple of things that strike me right away about Colson. One, he doesn't qualify anything he says in the course of the almost hour we spend together. He doesn't hesitate or waffle. This may be attributable to his education, or his years spent speaking publicly or doing interviews like these, or it might be that he just doesn't consider the other side of things. Rather, I think it's because he's thought about the other side and just knows what he thinks about things. This is refreshing. Two, Colson has, for lack of better terms, deeds and creeds, and isn't afraid to apologize for past wrongs.

"My generation has been very slow to learn to be humble about our faith," he says. "And we've had a hard time understanding that people don't always see things like we do. We tend to be judgmental. Martin Luther King said 'He whom ye would change you must first love.' The world needs to see that on our part, a lot better than my generation has done it. Francis Schaeffer said that 'the world will have the right to judge us by how we love one another.'"

I agree with Colson that the world needs to see it from my generation. Sadly, there seems to be a "you're either young, Reformed, and dogmatic or you're emergent" dichotomy forming, and it's troubling. I ask Colson how he would challenge my generation regarding church involvement.

"I have a passion for teaching people that there is truth and it's know-able," he says. "To understand that there's an organic connection between faith in Christ, and being part of a church. The relationship is spelled out so beautifully in Ephesians 5. Just as a husband and wife at the altar become one flesh, you meet Christ at the cross and leave as one with His church.

"I've seen much of the world where people could not get together for worship, and I've seen how desperate they were for fellowship, and how desperate they are for teaching and learning. Church isn't something to be endured, it's something to be entered into joyfully. Maybe you don't like the sermons, or maybe the music bothered you one Sunday, but those things are trivial compared to the very act of committing yourself to being part of the body of Christ, and participating fully."

Colson's description of prison church reminds me of a more intensified version of the persecution Christians deal with on secular campuses. I felt this acutely when I transferred out of a small, Christian liberal arts college and finished at a large, state university. For the first time I, a Christian, was a minority in my classrooms, a fact which made camaraderie with my Christian classmates more intense, and more important. Having the courage to have church behind bars strikes me as truly revolutionary.

"We live in a therapeutic age where everything is measured by how much I get out of it," he continues. "The church ought to be measured by what we put into it for God and others. And we live in an era of rampant individualism. So in a very individualistic

"WE LIVE IN AN ERA OF RAMPANT INDIVIDUALISM.... THE WHOLE IDEA OF BEING A PART OF A COMMUNITY IS COUNTERCULTURAL."

culture, the whole idea of being a part of a community is countercultural. And it fits perfectly in the what's-in-it-for-me, narcissistic attitudes prevalent in American culture."

Isn't it a little bit ironic that we are publishing vast numbers of books about community, while at the same time we are publishing large volumes about dropping out of one's church in order to "do relationships" in a more organic way? We seem to be more interested in talking and reading about community than actually "doing" it.

"It's easy to be down on the church, and it's easy to find its faults,"

Colson adds, "but when you become a believer, you *are* the church."

I then make a not-small tactical error by asking Colson where he goes to church.

"I've always resented the phrase 'Where do you go to church?' I don't go to a church; I'm a member of a church. You don't ask where somebody 'goes' to a country club. I'm not talking about where you're going, I'm talking about where you plant your flag and say, 'This is where I'm a Christian.'"

Oops. There are so many things I want to ask him, but don't. I'd love to know what Richard Nixon was really like. I'd also love to know what prison

"WE NEED TO CLEAN OUR ACT UP," SAYS COLSON OF THE EVANGELICAL CHURCH. "BUT NEVER AT THE EXPENSE OF THE TRUTH."

was like for him, but I'm also interested in his early church experiences.

"I knew immediately that I belonged to a church even though I'd never been in one," he remembers. "I've learned a great deal in church. I've had great pastors. Just this Sunday I was struggling with some things and his sermon just hit me like a ton of bricks. It liberated me."

What makes great pastors great pastors?

"They have a love for people in the church. They have a heart for discipleship, and that's what makes them great pastors."

I'm struck that Colson is one of only a few evangelical "superstars" who is also, and has always been, a layperson. Albeit a unique one, in that he approached his religious study much like I imagine him approaching his legal/political career. He studied voraciously, decided what he believed, and then chose to get very publicly involved.

"Christianity is a formulation of propositions that have been revealed to us, and that we're not free to meddle with or we end up with liberalism. Not liberal Christianity. Liberalism. We need to clean our act up," says Colson of the evangelical church. "But never at the expense of the truth. Something is either truth or it isn't. It's not negotiable."

I'm especially interested in things about our act that we need to clean up, and ask Colson as much.

"The heavy-handed political approach will backfire on us," he says. "We need to be careful as far as how we engage in public debate. We can't marry one political party. I don't think the church should ever be in one party's hip pocket or the other. We need to be careful that we don't appear to be single-issue. While the issue of life is overarching and is certainly number one on my list, there are a lot of other issues as well that flow from that, and you can't read the Bible without feeling that concern for the poor and compassion for the poor, and for all people's human rights are of importance. My desire would be for people to see a much clearer picture of who we are."

We agree that the emergent church seems to have wed itself to the political left, and become just as, if not more, politically heavy-handed than its conservative brethren. The secret message of Jesus, at least according to Brian McLaren, seems to be left-leaning politics.

"It's not only that there's a left tilt, particularly in the emergent church, that's pretty evident, but it is never considered fashionable for young people to be attracted to conservatives," Colson says. "Young people are very utopian by nature. Conservatism is not nearly as exciting as some idealogical scheme hatched in some coffee house in the West Bank. They look at that (conservatism) as kind of backward and regressive.

"The other factor," he continues, "is that no matter what side of the spectrum you're on, when you react against something, you'll eventually take on the characteristics of what you're reacting against. It's a rule of human nature. A force, counterforce argument. So if I say I'm going to resist these people who are oppressive in the church, I become more oppressive than what I was initially opposing."

This scares me for a number of reasons. The first and most obvious being that I once wrote a book called *Why We're Not Emergent*, and if Colson's rule of human nature holds true then I will probably be writing a book with a title like *Soul Tsunami* or *A Generous Orthodoxy* or *Velvet Elvis* in a couple of years. Also obvious, though, is the way this rule has already played out in the far left of the emergent movement. By insisting that the church that has creeds, doctrines, and boundaries is oppressive, they actually may be doing as much to oppress orthodox Christianity in our culture as any number of traditionally "scary" groups of people.

I ask him what he tells inmates in his ministry to look for in churches. "Number one is a church that believes in and preaches the Bible," Colson replies. "Calvin said that the number one task of the church is to preach the gospel. Second, it should be a place where disciples are made. Is this a place where I'm going to be discipled and grow as a Christian? The classic marks of the church, at least to the reformers, were preaching the gospel, administering the sacraments, and number three, discipline. Discipline in terms of both holding people accountable and teaching."

Colson, for the record, is willing to admit that we're not hitting on all of those cylinders in most instances. "We've put recruitment ahead of repentance," he says. "Church is performance oriented.

"Most of the churches I've been at have been in prison," he explains. "I've seen wonderful camaraderie that those guys have because they're persecuted. Because they're looked down upon. Because the rest of the inmates look down on them."

Pastor Zach Bartels, thirty, from Judson Memorial Baptist Church in Lansing, Michigan, is showing me around the building, and in particular the church's not-unextensive collection of Jesus pictures. Bartels has one in his office, of an especially feminine-looking Jesus gazing skyward, illuminated by a little lightbulb that comes with the frame. In the youth-group room, there are three, and we decide they are "playoff hockey, mullet and beard Jesus," "Phillies third baseman circa 1985 Jesus," and "Anglo-surfer Jesus." I mention this mostly just because I found it funny, but also to let you know that Zach Bartels, pastor, has a sense of humor. He's also working hard to teach his congregation who Jesus is, and who He isn't.

Bartels has just spent a week in northern Michigan, doing very traditional Baptist church things like preaching at a church camp for middle schoolers. "This was much harder at thirty than it was at twenty-five," he remarks, a little exhausted from the week, but still willing to show me around.

"We're proud of this," he says, opening the door to a clothing bank that occupies most of the church's basement. The Love Clothing Center opened in 1989 and has since clothed over 21,000 Lansing children. There are racks and racks of clothing, given for free to needy children and teenagers in the area. The program is run by Bartels' congregants, but is, as he says, "ecumenical," bringing together a number of churches in urban Lansing for the project. This is appropriate, as the church once served as a mission Sunday school for children of General Motors workers on Lansing's south side in the 1920s. Today it is part of the south side's urban sprawl. And this is not a charming, gentrified, urban sprawl. It's an ugly, concrete, Mountain Dew– and–cigarettes urban sprawl. This isn't the kind of place people get excited about when they get excited about doing urban ministry. This is sort of that nasty "middle ground"—not quite "inner-city" but definitely light-years away from suburbia. Hence my interest in Bartels—a young, talented musician/

pastor/scholar who could probably be somewhere else.

His church is small, around 150 people, but it's actually more diverse than almost any I've seen in a couple of years' worth of church research. There are honest-to-goodness old people here, but there's also a row or two worth of teenagers, and a handful of teens with electric guitars are up on the stage with Zach, in a suit, who is yowling through a version of "Awesome God" and then "In Christ Alone." The older folks in the congregation—actually everybody in the congregation—get through the songs because they know that "guitar hour" is a way for Zach to connect with and minister to the kids who share the stage with him.

Two other random things I like about small, Baptist churches. First, the children's message. This is the portion of the service where Zach calls all of the kids up to the front, and gives them a brief message before they file out for Sunday school. I also like the bulletins at these little churches. They all come from the same bulletin clearinghouse and feature pictures on the front which usually involve sun streaming through the clouds, along with a Bible verse. There's no objective reason for liking these, other than they remind me of my grandmother, and I love my grandmother and her old, little Baptist church.

Bartels preaches to the adults this morning from Luke 9:1–9, which gives Jesus' instructions to the Twelve as He sent them out to preach the kingdom of God. Verses 3–5 read: "Take nothing for your journey—no staff, nor bag, nor bread, nor money; and do not have two tunics. And whatever house you enter, stay there, and from there depart. And wherever they do not receive you, when you leave that town shake off the dust from your feet as a testimony against them."

"Jesus had guidelines for how these disciples would minister in this context," says Bartels, "it was already institutional! God forbid." I know he includes that joke for us.

Another thing about Zach's congregants: They're unbelievably friendly. I'm sure, in some sense, we represented "fresh meat"—a young couple with a child, showing interest in their church—but I can tell their kindness transcends recruitment. These people are just really, really nice.

The Luke passage also reminds us that we're not self-sufficient in ministry. Jesus sends the disciples out, giving them His power, but with a reminder that they are to rely on Him. The picture Jesus paints of missions is vastly different from the corporatized version we may see today, where some missionaries are prepped in boardroom suit-and-tie fundraising techniques.

What's also interesting about this passage, Bartels points out, is that Jesus only advocates "wiping the dust from his feet" of those who reject the gospel. Revolutionary types light onto the part of Jesus' ethos that had Him dining with prostitutes, sinners, and tax collectors, which is, of course, a good and important part of His ethos. Also important is this edge, or boundary. "In essence He's

THERE'S NO RISK-TAKING ON BEHALF OF THE GOSPEL.

saying that we're no longer wiping dust off our feet because we're Jews leaving a Gentile town, but because we're Christians," Bartels explains of the symbolic, formerly Jewish custom.

This also implies that rejection is going to be a part of our lives as believers. Not everybody is going to like us, or our message, which flies in the face of most of the pragmatic church models that have been around since the early 1980s, in which being liked (and thus, being attended) is the highest value. No less pragmatic is the "revolutionary" leave-your-church-and-find-God movement, which in effect says, "If people in your life don't like the church, fine; just distance yourself from the church and do your own spirituality."

The problem with this is that it is entirely self-sufficient. There's no risk-taking on behalf of the gospel. It allows us, like Barna's golfing CEO, to take with us our staff, bread, bag, extra tunic, and reputation.

✱ ✱ ✱

I really don't want to like College Church in Wheaton, Illinois. One reason is its name. I like churches that have names that reveal something about their position, names like Third *Presbyterian* or New Life *Reformed*, or Grace United *Methodist*, or Judson Memorial *Baptist*, or Upland Evangelical *Mennonite*. The other reason is that I don't want to like Wheaton, the suburb. I have a mental picture of it as a place where everyone makes more money than I do (not exactly true, but mostly), is better looking than I am (probably true), and went to Wheaton College (not necessarily) which is known on the Christian college circuit as "The Harvard[1] of the Midwest" or where you go when your dad is a famous Christian something.

That, and the stifling humidity, combine to make my attitude something less than tip-top as we walk to College Church with my wife's brother and his wife. I think the thing that I perceive about big, affluent churches is that they only care about catering to the whims of their affluent clientele, or, if they do venture outside the walls to do ministry, it's often something big, sexy, and public.[2] That (my ignorance) is one reason why today is so humbling.

Yes, the clientele at College Church is largely affluent. The uniform seems to be the Ivy-leagueish chinos-plus-shirt-plus-tie-plus-dark, navy sportcoat. But on the walk over, my brother-in-law, in a very disarmingly unintentional way, pointed out all of the immigrant populations in apartment buildings that are served by various college church ministries. Dark-skinned people banging out rugs over apartment-building railings. Dark-skinned children playing on crummy apartment-building toys.

And then he told me about a disabilities ministry, called STARS, that nearly brought tears to my eyes. The ministry's key verse is found in 1 Corinthians 12:21–22 and reads: "The eye cannot say to the hand, 'I don't need you!' And the head cannot say to the feet, 'I don't need you!' On the contrary, those parts of the body that seem to be weaker are indispensable" (NIV).

The ministry provides small-group Bible studies, Sunday school classes, and music ministry opportunities for hundreds of people with disabilities living in the Wheaton area, as well as a respite care ministry designed to give a break to caregivers. In almost twenty-five years of evangelical life, it's the first time I've seen or heard of anything[3] this intentional, well executed, and effective as an outreach toward disabled folks and their families. It makes me proud to be a Christian.

Dawn Clark, the director of disabilities outreach at College Church, has been working in some capacity (first volunteering, now full-time) with the ministry since the late 1990s when she and her husband returned stateside from the mission field.

"A developmental impairment does not make one unworthy to be taught and made a disciple," says Clark. "People talk about sanctity-of-life issues, and I think this has been a great way to welcome people into the body of Christ."

Clark admits that sometimes evangelical churches struggle with the balance between word and deed. And we both agree that big, affluent churches like College Church can appear, at first glance, to be so upscale, successful, comfortable, and white that they're not interested in reaching out.

"I really feel like this ministry helps people to see beyond the externals at our church," she says. "We live in the affluent, western suburbs. We live in Wheaton. We're right in the middle of Wheaton College. Of course we're going to reflect that to a certain extent. But this is a giving, serving, and working people. And this ministry started because of one woman's response to the Word of God."

The ministry began in the late 1960s when a woman in the church named Jean Hooten saw a child with a developmental disability and was saddened that there was nothing there for him to do. She lobbied the elders and was eventually given a Sunday school room.

"By the 1970s we have a picture on the front steps of the church of about ten kids and young adults," says Clark of the only artifact she could find to track the ministry's growth. The ministry now sees over fifty children and young adults in its Friday night meeting, and serves about eighty area families. Clark, who previously served as a Bible translator and physical therapist with her husband in Papau New Guinea, has been on board since 2002. She tells her own story of a call to the mission field to translate Scripture after growing up in a legalistic church setting.

"I saw God as a severe father waiting for you to screw up," she explains. "But through the reading of Scripture I came to understand grace and what it means to live in grace. I wanted to give that gift to others through translation, and when we came back to the states when our sons were in college I really didn't want to stay here."

Clark still had her license to work as a physical therapist, and when college bills began to mount, went back to work primarily with developmentally disabled children and their families. Eventually Clark was presented the opportunity to consider a position with College Church's disability ministry.

"I really felt God saying 'look at this.' I felt as strong a call as I'd first felt for Bible translation."

Now she manages the day-to-day aspects of the ministry, including a fund designed to help families with disabled children defer costs, and structuring the church's programs so that these families can be fully included in the life and body of the church. But the nature of her work, and the ministry, is always fluid and changing.

"Recently we were working with a family who has two children with autism," she says. "We asked the parents what they needed most and they just said 'sleep.' We told the father that we'd like to watch their kids and get them a hotel room for the night so that they could just rest, talk, and pray, and the man broke down in tears. And I thought to myself, 'This is why I love my church.'"

✳ ✳ ✳

It's been a great day in my hometown of Hartford City, Indiana (population: 7,000), where nobody knows anything about postmodernism, "revolutionaries," or how cool it is to be put out with the church. It's a city where I'm known more for graduating from Blackford High in 1994 than writing a book about the emergent church. I spent the afternoon with my dad watching semipro football, which is, if given the choice, what I'd pretty much like to do more than anything else on any given day. We both played semipro football in our respective eras, and there's something very relaxing about sitting on metal bleachers, watching other guys do what we still wish we could.

Now we're back home and turn on the Pro Football Hall of Fame induction speeches. Watching this kind of programming is not unlike watching the Academy Awards. It's basically really boring. It's a celebration of guys who have already been pretty widely celebrated, and the speeches are almost always too long. Yet here's former Washington Redskin wide receiver and 2008 inductee Art Monk, who quietly and passionately presents the gospel and quotes more Scripture than most American pastors during his speech.

Monk's words are something of a revelation. He begins by explaining that football and the Hall of Fame induction don't define him. Rather, he says, he is defined by his faith in Christ. "My identity and security," he says, "is found in the Lord. And what defines me and my validation comes in having accepted His Son Jesus Christ as my personal Savior. And what defines me is the Word of God, and it's the Word of God that will continue to shape and mold me into the person that I know that He's called me to be."

Interesting that Monk is on the cusp of joining a club that every football player in the world yearns to be defined by, yet he chooses instead to be defined by his membership in God's church, and articulates a stronger, more orthodox view of Scripture than a good many of today's Christian authors, speakers, and visionaries. It occurs to me that this is why I love football players—their ability to be completely honest and unflinching in moments of huge public importance.

He continues: "There's a Scripture that I think about almost every day and I've come to personalize to my life. It says: 'Lord who am I that you are mindful of me?' But if I'm going to boast, I'm going to boast today in the Lord, for it's because of Him that I'm here and I give Him thanks and glory and honor for all that He has done for me."

Monk not only quotes Scripture, but he does so in an evenhanded, humble way, which is a contrast to most cringe-worthy Christian-athlete rhetoric that seems devoid of any doctrine other than God-as-cosmic-good-luck-charm. It's a way that suggests that Monk has sat under good biblical and doctrinal teaching the majority of his adult life.

He was introduced by his son, James Monk Jr.,[4] who spoke at length about Monk's involvement in his local church body in Washington, D.C., and how his commitment to Christ shaped his career, and his parenting:

"So to answer the question, do you want to be like Art Monk when you grow up, my answer is I'd rather be like Dad. Dad, thank you for being the man of God that God has called you to be, and for raising me in the same way. As your best friend, as your admirer, as your biggest fan, and as your son, I want to tell the whole world that I love you and I'm truly honored and blessed to induct you into the 2008 Pro Football Hall of Fame."

I'm watching this with my own father, and my son is a few feet away from us on the floor, oblivious. What we don't say is that I know my dad hopes that I feel the same way about him (I do), and what I secretly hope, but don't say, is that one day my son will think and feel those things about me—not in an egotistical way, but in a way that suggests that they're true.

NOTES

1. There are several other Christian colleges who informally refer to themselves as the "Harvard" of something. These include Westmont College (California) and Calvin College (Michigan).
2. Missions trips to Africa or something of the sort.
3. Since my conversation with Dawn Clark, I've learned about several other churches that do similar ministries and do them well, although College Church was still one of the earliest to pioneer this type of outreach.
4. Art Monk's full name is James Arthur (Art) Monk.

Yet she on earth hath union

With God the Three in One,

And mystic sweet communion

With those whose rest is won:

O happy ones and holy!

Lord give us grace that we,

Like them, the meek and lowly,

On high may dwell with thee.

"The Church's One Foundation," verse 6

CHAPTER 7

THE CHURCH OF DIMINISHING DEFINITION

Y ou would be hard-pressed to find an evangelical thinker over the past fifty years more respected than John Stott. His preaching is exemplary. His commentaries are clear. His commitment to missions and the global church are beyond reproach. And his theology is always balanced.

That's why the following, from Stott's recent book *The Living Church: Convictions of a Lifelong Pastor*, is all the more striking: "I trust that none of my readers is that grotesque anomaly, an unchurched Christian. The New Testament knows nothing of such a person. For the church lies at the very centre of the eternal purpose of God."[1]

I imagine Stott considered this to be a pretty ordinary observation. After all, since at least the third century, Christians of all stripes have held to Cyprian's dictum: *extra Ecclesiam nulla salus* ("outside the Church there is no salvation"). Granted, Protestants have not used the phrase in the same way as Catholics and Orthodox. But the general principle has certainly been affirmed from Martin Luther on down through the Protestant tree.[2] Calvin famously argued that for those to whom God "is Father the church may also be Mother."[3] And the Westminster Confession states that "the visible church . . . is the kingdom of the Lord Jesus Christ, the house and family of God, out of which there is no ordinary possibility of salvation."[4] Stott is simply reflecting the broad consensus of Christian history when he calls the unchurched Christian a "grotesque anomaly."

If George Barna is correct, this consensus about indispensability of the church is unraveling right before our eyes. The church is no longer where we run to in order to be saved, but, we are told, where we must run from if we are to truly find God. Not only is the church ancillary to God's plans, it may actually get in the way of the kingdom. In that case, leaving the church is one very viable option. If the logic is true, there is simply no theological rationale that requires Christians to identify with the visible church. *Extra Ecclesiam* whatever.

WE OBJECT

There are two different kinds of theological objections to the necessity of the church—not always neatly separated objections, but not exactly the same either. The first says Christians don't need to belong to a visible church. By virtue of the Spirit and faith in Jesus, every Christian will belong to the invisible church, but identifying with a local expression of Christ's body is simply not necessary, and in some cases may be detrimental to the faith.

The second kind of objection has to do with the kind of church to which we must belong. People in this second category say, "Yeah, I still do church, but I've just left the institutional, cultural baggage behind.[5] I still fellowship with other believers as we follow after God together. So I'm still a part of a church, just not how traditionalists think of it." The first group says belonging to a visible body is not necessary. The second group doesn't argue that it's unnecessary (though sometimes that seems to be implied); they just have a much more organic, minimalist view of what constitutes church.

OBJECTION 1: CHURCHLESS CHRISTIANITY

The first objection argues for the legitimacy of churchless Christianity. The debate over "churchless Christianity" has been a hot topic among missiologists since the publication of Herbert Hoefer's book by the same name in 1991. The debate in missions is whether Hindus and Muslims who never identify with visible Christianity can nevertheless follow Jesus while staying in their respective communities. Can someone say yes to Jesus and no to the visible church?[6]

In many contexts there are cultural connotations with Christianity and the organized church that make saying yes to the church more difficult than saying yes to Jesus. Hindus may think that Christians are disrespectful because they do not take off their shoes during worship services, they sit on pews instead of the floor, and some of the Christian women no longer wear bangles. Muslims often associate Christianity with America's loose moral culture. Postmodern Westerns have a hard time aligning themselves with any institution, particularly one with such a checkered past (and present) as the church. Wouldn't is just be easier to take Jesus without the church?

Six Arguments *Against* a Churchless Christianity

In an article entitled, "The Challenge of Churchless Christianity: An Evangelical Assessment," missiologist Timothy Tennent makes several good arguments against the notion of churchless Christianity.[7] First, Tennent mentions the Nicene Creed and its confession, "I believe in one, holy, *catholic*, apostolic church" (emphasis added). *Catholic* reminds us of the universality of the church, that despite all our differences there is still one Lord, one faith, and one baptism (Eph. 4:5). If Christians are not baptized in the triune name and are not willing to identify with the visible Christian community, what happens to the orthodox confession in one catholic church? Second, we have the record of church history. "From a historical perspective, the existence of unbaptized believers in Christ who are not under the authority of the church is not accepted as normative ecclesiology."[8] Third, Tennent notes that the very word *ekklesia* means "public assembly" and speaks to the necessity of our Christian commitment being made visible.

Tennent offers three further arguments against a churchless Christianity. Argument four: We don't need to choose between no church and a thoroughly Westernized church. Or to put it in our context, we don't need to reject the church outright just because we don't like organs, praise bands, or big buildings. Argument five: Without church membership there's no place for the important role of church discipline. And finally, if Christians, especially those in other parts of the world, refuse to identify with the visible church, the whole church will be robbed of the insights and beauty that come from multivaried expressions of our common faith.

Relationships Are Not Enough

In the runaway bestseller *The Shack*, the Jesus character explains that he doesn't like religion and he doesn't create institutions.[9] The church we see is only a man-made system. The church I came to build, Jesus tells us, is "all about relationships and simply sharing life."[10] But are relationships enough? Can the church remain invisible as an organized entity so long as we love God and love each other? Is it possible, as Brian Sanders argues, for

Christians to be so committed to the invisible church that they need to leave the visible church on principle?[11] In short, do we need to see the church or can we just be the church?

Part of the confusion lies with the familiar distinction between the visible and invisible church. Most people think of the invisible church as the community of saints from all times and all places. The visible church, on the other hand, is the organized fellowship that you can see with your eyes and probably meets for worship in a building every Sunday. While this popular distinction has its place, it oversimplifies the invisible-visible dimension of the church.

The invisible church can also refer to the church hidden, and the visible church to the church manifest.[12] That is, the invisible church is the church we believe in by faith, the church in communion with God, the church that partakes in all Christ's benefits, the glorious church yet to be fully revealed.[13] By contrast, much of this glory is hidden in the visible church. Instead of beauty, we see imperfection. We see a community often unlike Christ. We see the church with little "already" and a lot of "not yet."

Think about the ramification of this sharpened understanding of the visible and invisible church. Instead of using the invisible-visible distinction as a way to avoid church commitment, church-leavers would see the distinction as an impetus for patience with the church. With this more careful understanding, we'd be more like the Reformers who never used the distinction to undermine the place of the organized church, but to emphasize the spiritual essence of God's gathered people.

This spiritual essence needs to be made visible. As the body of Christ, the church makes visible our invisible God. "The Body of Christ takes up space on earth," argued the German martyr Dietrich Bonhoeffer. "The Body of Christ can only be a visible Body, or else it is not a Body at all."[14] Barna would have "Revolutionaires"—his term for those who have joined the "revolution" of churchless Christianity—demonstrate the presence of God wherever they are rather than be drawn "out of the world and into a relationship with an institution."[15]

CHURCHLESS CHRISTIANITY MAKES ABOUT AS MUCH SENSE AS A CHRISTLESS CHURCH, AND HAS JUST AS MUCH BIBLICAL WARRANT.

But what if we are meant to demonstrate the presence of God in the world by joining a visible institution? Again Bonhoeffer: "The Body of Christ becomes visible to the world in the congregation gathered round the Word and Sacrament."[16] Without the institutional church there may be less to despise about Christianity, but there would also be more of an invisible bride to love and less of a visible Christ to see. "Theologically, we have been discovering anew that the Church is not an appendage to the Gospel," says missiologist Stephen Neill, "it is itself a part of the Gospel. The Gospel cannot be separated from that new people of God in which its nature is to be made manifest."[17]

The church is unique. Though individual believers are indwelt with the Holy Spirit as temples of God, only the church constitutes the body of Christ. One church-leaver argues that many of the premises of institutional Christianity are suspect "given this one cold, hard fact: Christ indiscriminately, fully, and equally establishes his presence and life within every believer."[18] While it is true that Christ establishes life in every believer, the church alone is "the fullness of him who fills all in all" (Eph. 1:23). Churchless Christianity makes about as much sense as a Christless church, and has just as much biblical warrant. John Stott's assessment of evangelism in the book of Acts is right: The Lord "didn't add them to the church without saving them, and he didn't save them without adding them to the church. Salvation and church membership went together; they still do."[19]

OBJECTION 2: NEW WINE, NO WINESKINS

If the first kind of objection argues for the legitimacy of churchless Christianity, the second kind of objection seeks to redefine what it means to be a part of a church. Barna explains:

> The small *c* church refers to the congregation-based faith experience, which involves a formal structure, a hierarchy of leadership, and a specific group of believers. The term *Church*, on the other hand, refers to all believers in Jesus Christ, comprising the population of heaven-bound individuals who are connected by their faith in Christ, regardless of their local church connections or involvement. . . . As you will see, the Revolution is designed to advance the Church and to redefine the church.[20]

Elsewhere Barna adds "It's not about *church*. It's about *the Church*."[21]

"Revolutionaries" don't see themselves as antichurch. They are *anti-church-as-we-know-it*. By their understanding, the church equals the people in the church, so you can no more hate the church than hate yourself. Church is not a place you go to, but a way of living in relationship to God and to His followers. So, according to church-leavers, we cannot abandon church because church is something we are.[22] Church simply refers to those who live in community and try to live out the teachings of Jesus.[23]

In other words, *church* is plural for *Christian*. Where two or three believers are together, encouraging one another in their journey with God, that's church no matter the geographical location.[24] Tony Jones provides a typical anti-church-as-we-know-it explanation of the famous Matthew 18 passage about where two or three are gathered: "Christians have, in principle, claimed that nothing more is required to constitute a church than a couple of believers on a park bench. Yet the vines of bureaucracy and hierarchy have snaked their way around God's people for centuries, often choking out innovation and progress."[25]

Church is what two believing friends do when they talk about Jesus at Starbucks. You and your Christian buddies who never go to worship services and are under no ecclesiastical authority, by virtue of living in community and trying to live like Jesus, constitute a church just as much as First Reformed or Harvest Fellowship.[26] It's no surprise, then, to hear from one church-leaver that there are "an endless number of ways" to conceive of and practice being the church.[27] All you need are two or more Christians in the same place at the same time being spiritual together.

THIS NEW ECCLESIOLOGY ARGUES THAT A CHURCH CAN BE FREE FROM STRUCTURE, REGULAR WORSHIP SERVICES, AND RELIGION.

The problem with this minimalist ecclesiology is that it confuses definition and function. I have no problem with defining the church as elect people of God, or as the gathered Christian community, or as all those who have put their faith in Jesus. These are pretty standard definitions. But to say the church is the people of God is not the same as saying that wherever the people of God are there you have a church. The problem with the previous sentence is that "church" is used in two different ways. At the beginning of the sentence, "the church" refers to the universal, organic fellowship of Christians. So, of course, the church is the people of God. The two are almost synonymous. But in the second half of the sentence, "a church" suggests a local, concrete expression of the universal, organic fellowship. The church manifests itself in churches. And churches do certain things and are marked by certain characteristics.

So as a definition, *the church* may be the people of God, but for God's people gathered to be *a church* they must function in certain way. When Paul wrote his letters to local churches, he wasn't addressing three Christian guys who shared an apartment and talked about the spirituality of Euripides. He was writing to a group of Christians who embraced a certain structure, participated in a certain kind of worship service, and shared a certain kind of doctrinal and ethical standard. This made their gathering a church and not just an exercise in hanging out.[28]

The "revolutionary" understanding of the church is right in what it affirms—namely, that *ekklesia* refers to the people of God—but wrong in all that it leaves out. Specifically, this new ecclesiology argues that a church can be (1) free from structure, (2) free from regular worship services, and (3) free from religion. I'm not suggesting that everyone criticizing the church agrees with all three of these statements. "Revolutionary" theology does not tend to be that well established, or frankly, that well thought out. The new ecclesiology does not spend much time explicitly formulating a doctrine of the church. Rather, the new ecclesiology carries with it a host of assumptions that allow church-leavers to redefine the church to their minimalist liking.

Decently and in Order

The first assumption is that the church does not need structure. As one couple puts it, "Over the years, we have discovered there is an inverse relationship between Spirit (divine) and structure (human)."[29] Similarly, Jones argues that "church should function more like an open-source network and less like a hierarchy or bureaucracy"[30] And in *The Shack*, the Jesus character announces, "Hierarchy imposes laws and rules and you end up missing the wonder of relationship that we intended for you."[31] The idea is that church can exist, and it seems *should* exist, without authority structures or any role distinctions among its members.

There are only two problems with this model of church: it's unbiblical and it's unrealistic. "Anarchy does not work," writes Professor Herman Bavinck.

"To say that Christ has founded a church without any organization, government, or power is a statement that arises from principles characteristic of philosophical mysticism but takes no account of the teaching of Scripture, nor of the realities of life."[32] Granted, no one wants a church run by dictators or egomaniacs, just as no one wants a church where relationships are choked out by policies and procedures. But the Bible simply does not teach a leaderless church. Instead we see the apostles exercising great authority over the churches (e.g., 2 Cor. 13:1–4). We have pastors commanded to "exhort and rebuke with all authority" (Titus 2:15; see also 2 Tim. 4:2). We see elder rule (Acts 14:23; 15:2; 20:17; 1 Tim. 3:1–7; 5:17; Titus 1:5; James 5:14; 1 Peter 1:1; 5:1), accompanied by the office of deacon to care for the physical needs of the congregation (1 Tim. 3:8–13; Phil. 1:1; see also Acts 6:1–7). To be sure, elders are not to domineer over those in their charge, but they still must exercise oversight (1 Peter 5:2–3), and those in the congregation should "obey your leaders and submit to them, for they are keeping watch over your souls, as those who will have to give an account" (Heb. 13:17).

Similarly, much of the anti-church-as-we-know-it literature harbors a strong bias against pastors. As a group, pastors are certainly not above criticism, but the office itself is not to blame. After all, "it was [Christ] who gave some to be apostles, some to be prophets, some to be evangelists, and some to be pastors and teachers (Eph. 4:11 NIV). We cannot throw out the pastoral office just because we prefer a "flat structure"[33] or just because some pastors are goons. Pastoral ministry is what God has entrusted to the elders of the church (Acts 20:28; 1 Peter 5:1–2).

Just as important, the role of pastor is steeped in rich biblical imagery. In the book *Shepherds after My Own Heart: Pastoral Traditions and Leadership in the Bible*, Timothy Laniak presents a careful biblical study of pastor/shepherd leadership. He observes that shepherds are protectors, providers, and guides whose main responsibility is care for the well-being of the sheep.[34] Pastors must exercise "the benevolent use of authority. . . . Authority without compassion leads to harsh authoritarianism. Compassion without authority leads to social chaos."[35] This is a much more balanced and more biblical look at pastoral ministry than the "all or nothing," "tyrannical authority or no authority" dichotomies promoted by some contemporary authors.[36]

Besides being biblical, leadership structures are just plain inevitable. Reflecting on the early church, Wayne Meeks writes, "No group can persist for any appreciable time without developing some patterns of leadership, some differentiation of roles among its members, some means of managing conflict, some ways of articulating shared values and norms, and some sanctions to assure acceptable levels of conformity to those norms."[37] Someone needs to adjudicate disputes. Someone or some group must have the final say.

Even in a unit as small and organic as the family, there are authority structures. Mom and Dad make the rules, with Dad leading the way. In a good home, there will be struc-

> **THE CHURCH, AS THE ELECT PEOPLE OF GOD, IS BOTH ORGANISM AND ORGANIZATION. THE CHURCH IS A MATURING, LIVING THING.**

tures and routines. Chores will be divvied up. Curfews will be set. Bills will be paid on a certain day. Meals will happen around a certain time. Every home has lots of rules, written and unwritten, and lots of decision-making patterns that help bring some measure of order out of chaos.

The same is true for the household of faith. I don't like Robert's Rules of Order any more than the next guy, but sometimes you need them. I prefer to lead our elders meetings by consensus, and usually I can. But when we just can't agree, I'll lead us through the cumbersome process of making motions, seconds, amendments, call the question, etc. It's not sexy, but it's one way to make sure people get heard and a decision gets made.

No church will get it all right or strike the balance between form and freedom in a way that makes everyone happy. But most policies happen for a reason. We had to write up a van policy because once our church bought a van we had to decide who could use it, when, and for what purposes. It sounds wonderful to say, "Let's do away with bureaucracy and business meetings and we'll all just share the van," but in real life four hundred people don't just share vans. Some leave it a mess or leave the tank empty. Some are careful drivers and others are reckless. Some uses take priority over others and on and on. You get the point. And this is just one example of dozens of issues that come up in a church. In Paul's day it was widows (1 Tim. 5:3–16). In our day it's van policies, child safety laws, personnel handbooks, small-group leader training, and a hundred other things that need order, structure, and governance.

The church, as the elect people of God, is both organism and organization. The church is a breathing, growing, maturing, living thing. It is also comprised of a certain order (1 Cor. 14:40), with institutional norms (5:1–13), doctrinal standards (15:1–2), and defined rituals (11:23–26). The two aspects of the church—organism and organization—must not be played off against each other, for both are "grounded in the operations of the glorified head of the church through the Holy Spirit."[38] Offices and gifts, governance and the people, organization and organism—all these belong together. They are all blessings from the work of Christ.[39]

God could rule His church in a different way, but He chose to use means. We see throughout the Bible the "divine preference for human agency."[40] The antichurch crowd understands this when it comes to the world, but they have little patience for it when it comes to the church. They pit Spirit against structure, Christ's care against pastoral care, and God's authority against human authority. Bonhoeffer was right: "The Church or congregation is an articulated organism. When we speak of the Church as the Body of Christ, we include its articulation and order. These are essential to the Body and are of divine appointment. An unarticulated body is doomed to perish... Church order is divine both in origin and character, though of course it is meant to serve and not to rule."[41]

Be the Church As the Church

The second assumption behind the new ecclesiology is that the church does not need regular worship services. Of course, they would say we need to worship, but we can do that in a bar or at the park as well (or better) than in a church building on Sunday morning.[42] The weekly worship service is derided as a boring performance full of passive spectators, a dull lecture, and meaningless routines. "The Revolution," says Barna, "is about recognizing that we are not called to *go* to church. We are called to *be* the church."[43] Elsewhere he maintains, "Worship is not an event I attend or a process I observe; it is the lifestyle I lead."[44]

Barna is right on principle. Worship as a lifestyle is good and biblical (Rom. 12:1–2), as is being the church (assuming that is a convoluted way of saying "act like Christians"). But what about our actions? Does part of *being* the church entail worshiping together *as* the church? It's true that a church is more than the sum of its worship services. But a church that does not assemble regularly for corporate worship is not a church. Worship services are not peripheral to the life of the church.

We need to recapture a broader vision for what we are doing on Sunday morning. We are not coming together for a few songs and an ill-conceived oration. Our gathering for worship is an exercise in covenant renewal, a weekly celebration of the resurrection, and a foretaste of the heavenly banquet to come.

The New Testament strongly suggests that the two go together: Those who are the church take time to worship as the church. We know from Acts 2:42 that the first Christians met together regularly for teaching, fellowship (possibly the word for taking a collection), the Lord's Supper, and prayer. We know from 1 Corinthians 12–14 that public worship was an important part of the life of the church. We see in 1 Timothy 4:13 that there were regular times for the public reading of Scripture. In 1 Corinthians 11:18 we read instructions for "when you come together as a church," indicating that there was a unique gathering "as a church" that was not the same as a few Christians hanging out and talking about Jesus. As Gordon Fee puts it, "The people of God may be called the 'church/assembly' first of all because they regularly assemble as a 'church/assembly.'"[45] Later in 1 Corinthians 16 we read instructions for setting aside a collection "on the first day of every week," suggesting that the church at Corinth met for services of worship every Sunday. And in Hebrews 10:25 we are commanded not to neglect to meet together (literally, do not forsake the assembly of yourselves). The word for "meet together," *episyna-gogen*, does not refer to Christian friends reading their Bibles together but to the formal gathering of God's people for worship.[46] So, no, you can't stop going to church and still be the church.

And what about the role of preaching in church worship? From all I've read and heard about church-leavers, the main thing they are "escaping" is the sermon. Most people leaving church still see the need for some kind of community. We shouldn't think most of them as interested in lone-ranger Christianity. Often, these ex-churchgoers meet together for prayer, account-ability, and encouragement. They may even sing songs, read Scripture, and share some thoughts on God. But the one thing conspicuous in its absence is the sermon. Preaching is nothing but "hiding behind a big pulpit, dressed up in holy robes, preaching holy words to a faceless crowd and then disappearing into an office" says one leader in the house-church movement.[47] Today's sermon, according to Frank Viola, has "no root in Scripture," was "borrowed from pagan culture," and "detracts from the very purpose for which God designed the church gathering."[48] When church-leavers make their list of what is superfluous to church they put the sermon alongside such *adiaphora* (a theological term for actions not sanctioned nor prohibited by Scripture) as pulpits, stages, choirs, organs, information tables, stained glass windows, altar calls, and clap offerings.[49] They simply assume that preaching is not essential to biblical worship, and may even be detrimental to it.

But historically this has not been the case.[50] John Stott traces a sermonic thread from Jesus, to the apostles, through the writings of Justin

> **JOHN STOTT CONCLUDES THAT "PREACHING IS INDISPENSABLE TO CHRISTIANITY."**

Martyr, Tertullian, Irenaeus, and Eusebius; through the preaching of John Chrysostom, the Friars, and the Dominicans; through the Reformers, the Puritans, the Methodists, all the way down to contemporary evangelicals, and concludes that "preaching is indispensable to Christianity."[51]

For example, though Viola would have us believe that word-based ministry in the early church was always a free-flowing exchange of ideas, the *Didache* shows us otherwise. Dating to the beginning of the second century (or thereabouts), the *Didache*, or *The Teaching of the Twelve Apostles*, was akin to an early church constitution. From this document, we see the central role preaching played in the fledgling church. There were daily services of reading the Word, and a large body of prophets, teachers, bishops, and deacons devoted themselves full-time to preaching and teaching. In fact, "the *Didache* assumes that the main function of the various ministries is teaching."[52] The setting of the *Didache* presumes not just mutual sharing but designated leaders charged with authoritative teaching and preaching in the congregation.

The sermon was not stolen from the pagans or inherited from the enlightenment. It came from Judaism, which developed and refined the practice of exegesis and expositional preaching in the centuries leading up to Christ.[53] "We know," says Hughes Oliphant Old, "that in the time of Jesus the Torah, the Law of Moses, was regularly read and preached in worship. This was the cardinal characteristic of Jewish worship."[54] We can see this in nascent form throughout the Old Testament. The Levites were to teach Israel the law (Deut. 33:10). The true priest was not just a butcher but a teaching priest (2 Chron. 15:3). Ezra read the law to the returning exiles, "giving them the sense of it" (Neh. 8:6–8). And we see the same development in the New Testament. We know John the Baptist preached and Jesus preached. We know Paul preached and instructed his apprentice Timothy, with the most solemn warning, to also preach (2 Tim. 4:1–2). Even Jesus Himself, we should remember, was a trainer of preachers, sending His disciples out not just to facilitate group discussions but to preach (Mark 3:14). The apostles considered the ministry of the Word such a full-time job that they appointed other men to care for the physical needs of the church (Acts 6:1–7). Clearly, teaching and preaching were far from peripheral to the ministry of the early church.

So how can so many show such contempt for preaching when the Bible gives it such a privileged place? This under-appreciation for preaching comes from the ignorance of three theological truths.

First, church-leavers think of the traditional sermon as boring, modern monologue. But the early Christians, not to mention the Reformers, had a more corporate understanding of the ministry of the Word.[55] The preacher may have been the only one speaking (except for the occasional and welcome "amen"), but the time was still considered *corporate* worship because preacher and listener would exult in the Word together. The preacher worshiped as he spoke the Word and the congregation worshiped just as much to hear the Word. If our preaching seems like an oration or a simple lecture and the hearers see themselves as passive pew-warmers, then we are to blame, not the nature of preaching itself.

Second, church-leavers, and most churchgoers for that matter, have no concept of Christ being present in the preaching of the Word. God has always been a revealing God, a God who speaks to His people. By His words God created the heavens and the earth. By the word—spoken and then written—He formed the nation of Israel at Sinai. By the word declared—and written—He instructed His people through the prophets. By the Word He forms, gathers, and instructs the church.

> **GOD MEETS WITH AND RULES OVER HIS PEOPLE THROUGH THE AUTHORITATIVE PREACHING OF THE WORD OF GOD.**

Christ, the Word made flesh, is present in God's speech to His people. We see this expressed in the *Didache* where the Lord is said to be present where the things of the Lord are spoken,[56] and in 1 Peter 1 where the word of God is the Word of Scripture and, in a derivative but not less real sense, the preached sermon (1:25). God meets with and rules over His people, not through a facilitated experience of group sharing, but through the authoritative preaching of the Word of God.

This leads to the third neglected truth; namely, that preaching is proclamation. The Greek word for preacher is *kerux*. It is different than the word for *teacher* or *apostle* (2 Tim. 1:11). A *kerux* is a herald. He is not the leader of an inductive Bible study, as important as those are. He is not engaged in give-and-take dialogue, though there should be some of that in the church. And he is not to simply give testimony to what the Lord is doing in his life, though that can be good to hear. He is a herald, declaring a message for the

King. When Amos predicted a "famine" of "hearing the words of the Lord" (Amos 8:11) he wasn't thinking of the lack of personal conversations about Yahweh over a grande cup of goat's milk. He was thinking about the absence of God's appointed mouthpieces to declare His Word. If we lose preaching—the passionate, authoritative proclamation of God's message from God's man to God's people—we are losing more than a half hour talk once a week. We are losing a normative, essential aspect of Christian worship, one that began in the New Testament, stretches back into the Old, and has had a rich and continuous history over the past two thousand years.

The answer to bad preaching (and no doubt that's what we have in some of our churches) is not no preaching, but better preaching—preaching full of meat and marrow; preaching that manifestly comes out of the Scriptures and leads us back to them week after week; preaching that is unquestionably soaked in godliness and the presence of God; preaching delivered with passion and humility as from a dying man to dying men. When pastors preach like this, some will love it and some will not. But no one will have the right to label the sermon "a little talk" or "an inspiring oration."[57]

Religion Pure and Undefiled

The third assumption behind the new ecclesiology is that the church is free from religion. *Religion* is a tricky word. Some people use it like Tim Keller as a stand-in for legalism, appeasing God through ritual and good works.[58] If *religion* is code for pompous, self-justifying, insincere, moral do-gooders, then Jesus certainly came to abolish religion. Likewise, if "Jesus without religion"[59] means understanding Jesus apart from one's misunderstandings about Christianity and church baggage, then let's dump that religion too.

But *religion* hasn't always been a bad word. Jonathan Edwards used *religion* as a synonym for genuine Christian faith. According to the apostle James, religion can be either good or bad (1:26–27). At the popular level I think most people understand religion pretty well. Sure, there may be elements of works-righteousness in many people's conception of religion, but in general most people have a pretty good working definition of religion. Religion involves a set of beliefs, usually from a sacred book, with prescribed rituals and observances, and specific commands to obey. Granted, this doesn't get at the heart of true biblical religion, which is all about the heart. But this doesn't mean Christianity is not a religion.

It's popular to say that Jesus did not come to start a new religion or Jesus did not come to make people Christians.[60] Of course, on one level this is true. Jesus didn't see Himself in these anachronistic categories. But what most people mean when they pooh-pooh religion is that following Jesus is not the sort of thing that is bound by creeds and rules. "The Bible doesn't teach you to follow rules. It is a picture of Jesus" is how one book puts it. God doesn't want us to "look for rules and principles; look for relationship—a way of coming to be with us."[61] This is what is meant by religion-free faith: no rules, just relationships. "Faith," says Leonard Sweet, is "not ritual, dogma, religion, or spiritual weirdness. It's authentic experience made personal through our full participation in what God is doing."[62]

If faith is essentially a relationship without all the trappings of religion, then it's easy to see how church is construed as nothing but relationships too. But Christian faith is not without dogma. We are, after all, putting faith in something besides faith itself. And as for ritual, what about the Lord's Supper, baptism, or praying the prayer Jesus taught His disciples to pray? Christianity is a religion. We have a sacred book, sacred teaching, sacred ordinances, and sacred offices. Of course, I'd want to argue that Christianity is a very different kind of religion, unlike any other. What Christians mean by ritual, for example, is different than what a Buddhist means. But we are religious people.

And our churches should reflect our unique religious commitments. Relationships are indispensable, but not enough. No matter what the teachers of tickling ears say, we do have rules to follow. Jesus didn't say if you love Me you'll feel close to Me. He said if you love Me, you'll keep My commandments. The church, as the gathering of those who love Jesus, should be pure, holy, loving, and true—both as an indication of our obedience and as a reflection of the character of God. That's why discipline has traditionally been a mark of the church. Discipline promotes the purity of the church and vindicates the honor of the Lord Jesus Christ. Yet how can there be discipline without a church? How can there be accountability if church is not in any way an institution with standards and dogma, but only a gathering of two or more Christians in the park?

Christianity is not whatever we want it to be. It is, whether we like it or not, organized religion. And the church is what gives it its organization shape and definition. That's why people don't like the church. Sure, she's old, stale, and sinister at times. But the other reason—the main reason, I think—people don't like the church is because the church has walls. It defines truth, shows us the way to live, and tells us the news we must believe if we are to be saved.

"If only I could find a church without religion," you think to yourself, "then by golly, that would be the church for me." Except it wouldn't be a church at all.

One Last Caution and the Next Big Thing

It's no coincidence that several of the loudest church critics are advocates for the house-church movement. These trends are always hard to gauge, but my hunch is that house churches will be the next big thing in American Christianity.[63] They are (or at least seem to be) more relational, less institutional, more participatory, and more organic—all pluses for postmoderns.

There is, of course, biblical precedence for churches meeting in homes. So there's no reason for those in "normal" churches to freak out just because twenty people meet in a friend's home for church instead of two thousand people on forty acres off the highway. If house churches have good preaching, good leadership,

> **THERE IS, OF COURSE, BIBLICAL PRECEDENCE FOR CHURCHES MEETING IN HOMES.**

good theology, intentional discipleship, appropriate structures, rich worship, and administer the sacraments and practice church discipline, then I don't care if they meet in my basement. House churches aren't the only way to do church, but done right, they are *a* way.

But that's the key: House churches are *a* way, not *the* way to do church. Churches meeting in homes is not the problem. The problem is that "house church" in America often means anticlergy, antiauthority, antiliturgy, anti-sermon, antibuilding, anti–most ways of doing church over the past 1,700 years. "The nature of Church," writes one house-church proponent, "is not reflected in a constant series of religious meetings led by professional clergy in holy rooms specially reserved to experience Jesus, but in the prophetic way followers of Christ live their everyday life in spiritually extended families as a vivid answer to the questions society faces, at the place where it counts most: in their homes."[64] House-church advocates often argue that traditional church ignores real life and makes genuine relationships impossible. While regular churches are impersonal and institutionalized, house churches are informal and full of life.

In actuality, house churches, like other churches, have their strengths and weaknesses. As a graduate of Gordon-Conwell Theological Seminary,

I get their ministry magazine *CONTACT*. Recently there was an article by an anonymous graduate about the house-church movement in China. The author does a tremendous job, in just a few pages, of highlighting the strengths and weaknesses of the house-church movement. On the one hand, worship in a Chinese house church is "an indescribable experience."[65] Many are attracted to the inspiring worship experience and warm fellowship. "Joy and excitement permeate the room. Limited space and fear of the authorities create a closely knit, family fellowship." The house churches in China are vibrant and their growth has been explosive. In Beijing alone it's been estimated that between six thousand and ten thousand house churches have been planted in the last decade. The author believes the house-church movement in China "is a living, present day example of the first century early church."[66]

But the house-church movement is far from perfect. The house churches are "an organizational nightmare." Many times, no one knows who will be speaking or what the person's credentials are. Meeting times and locations are switched at the last minute. Church leadership is unstable. Churches often split or divide without adequate preparation. Biblical accountability is a challenge.

The house church in China can be a theological mess as well. "Just like the early church, the house church in China is prone to cult-like attacks and theological heresy." Cults "send undercover adherents into churches for months or even years before ousting the pastor and gaining control of the flock."[67] Congregations have a hard time distinguishing between heresy and orthodoxy. Moreover, the preaching is often weak, making it hard for the well educated (especially those who have attended church overseas) to adjust to the low quality of instruction in many house churches.

The author of the article mentions other weaknesses. House churches lack a visible presence in the community. Without a building, their churches seem to disappear during the week, especially in China where persecution drives the house-church movement underground. Lack of diversity is another problem. Most house churches attract college students and young professionals, but do not draw much from older persons. And without child care, families with small children rarely attend. Ministries for the youth are almost nonexistent. Finally, "probably most lacking in China's house churches is a 'longing for global worship.' In an open country, it is a privilege to experience a large worship service. House church worshipers in China long for this, a larger worship experience beyond their own small group." They long for "a larger, more diverse worshiping Body of Christ."[68]

Obviously, the house-church movement in America will be different from the one in China. We have more resources and more opportunities for training. Most significantly, we are not facing persecution. The house-church movement in China was not a reaction to megachurches or Constantine. The movement arose out of necessity. Persecution started the house-church movement, and the Lord continues to use persecution to help it grow. Persecution purifies the church and those who withstand the threat of persecution exhibit an authentic faith that attracts others. Without persecution, the house-church movement around the world will develop along very different lines, for better and for worse.

The point in this little excursus is not to belittle house churches, but to guard against idealism. There is no perfect church, nor is there one magically spiritual way of doing church. Christians need structure and spontaneity, form and freedom, rules and relationships. It's a sign of our weaknesses that so many are clamoring for less bureaucracy and more community in the church. It's a sign of their weakness that house churches in China are, out of necessity, beginning to develop organizational structures to better coordinate evangelism, missions, and training. Likewise, as we self-flagellate over having megachurches and having a mortgage, leaders in China "pray for the day of owning their own church building and moving toward a large church model."[69]

Every way of doing church and every context has its strengths and weaknesses. We all have things to learn and areas in which we need to grow. The one constant is that we all need Christ, His word, His Spirit, and, not least of all, His bride. If we are to make it in the world as a people and make a difference in the world as his people, we need the church. We need the church in visible manifest and sometimes hidden beauty. We need the church of individuals and of institutions. Most of all, we ought to love the church—in all her organic and organizational mess and glory.

NOTES

1. John Stott, *The Living Church* (Downers Grove, Ill.: InterVarsity, 2007), 19.
2. For a discussion of Luther's view of the church and the central place it held in his thinking, see Heiko A. Oberman, *Luther* (New York: Image Books, 1992), 246–58, 270–71.
3. John Calvin, *Institutes of the Christian Religion* (Louisville: Westminster John Knox, 1960), IV.i.1. Calvin seems to be alluding to Cyprian's line, "You cannot have God for your Father unless you have the church for your Mother."
4. *The Westminster Confession of Faith* (Suwanee, Ga.: Great Commission Publications, 1998).
5. For example, Jason Zahariades writes, "In order to be the Church, we need to leave the church. In other words, in order to truly become God's people as He intended, we must abandon our cultural version of organizational church"; "Detoxing from Church" in Spencer Burke, comp., *Out of the Ooze* (Colorado Springs, NavPress, 2007), 38.
6. This line comes from the Timothy Tennent's excellent book *Theology in the Context of World Christianity* (Grand Rapids: Zondervan, 2007), 194. In his chapter "Ecclesiology: Followers of Jesus in Islamic Mosques" (193–220), Tennent analyzes the C–1 to C–6 spectrum of contextualization. In particular, Tennent examines C–5 Muslims who accept Jesus as Lord and Savior but never self-identify as Christians. After careful evaluation, Tennent concludes that "one's religious identity with Jesus Christ should create a necessary rupture with one's Islamic identity, or else our identity in Jesus Christ would mean nothing" (217).

7. See Timothy C. Tennent, "The Challenge of Churchless Christianity: An Evangelical Assess-ment" *International Bulletin of Missionary Research*, vol. 29, no. 4, 171–76. The examples in the previous paragraph of Hindu and Muslim discomfort with organized Christianity also come from Tennent's fine article.

8. Ibid. Note: Because Tennent's article was accessed from the Internet, I cannot determine the original page numbers for this article.

9. William P. Young, *The Shack:* (Los Angeles: Windblown, 2007), 179. In the first nineteen months, 4.4 million copies of the book were distributed, according to the Public Relations Source, PR Newswire.

10. Ibid., 178.

11. Brian Sanders, *Life After Church* (Downers Grove, Ill., InterVarsity, 2007), 17.

12. See David Wells, *The Courage to be Protestant* (Grand Rapids: Eerdmans, 2008), 220ff.

13. Herman Bavinck, *Reformed Dogmatics: Holy Spirit, Church, and New Creation,* vol. 4 (Grand Rapids: Baker, 2008), 287–88.

14. Dietrich Bonhoeffer, *The Cost of Discipleship*, rev. ed. (1937; repr., New York: Mac-millan,1959), 277.

15. George Barna, *Revolution* (Carol Stream, Ill.: Tyndale, 2005), 127.

16. Bonhoeffer, *The Cost of Discipleship*, 281.

17. As quoted in Trueblood, *The Incendiary Fellowship*, 28.

18. Jim Palmer, *Divine Nobodies*, 85.

19. Stott, *The Living Church*, 32.

20. Barna, *Revolution*, x.

21. Ibid., 38. Emphasis in original.

22. Jacobsen, "Why I Don't Go to Church Anymore," 182.

23. Sarah Cunningham, *Dear Church* (Grand Rapids: Zondervan, 2006), 11, 112. See also Frank Viola, "The Deep Ecclesiology of the Body" in Burke, *Out of the Ooze*, 102; Neil Cole, *Organic Church* (San Francisco: Jossey-Bass, 2005), 53. It's worth noting that Friedrich Schleiermacher, the father of Protestant Liberalism, offered a similar definition of the church: "The Christian church takes shape though the coming together of regenerate individuals to form a system of mutual interaction and cooperation." (Quoted in Bavinck, *Reformed Dogmatics*, 295).

24. Palmer, *Divine Nobodies*, 84, 86.

25. Tony Jones, *The New Christians*, 191. See also Jaeson Ma, *The Blueprint*, 205. To their credit, Viola and Barna admit that this passage is about church discipline (*Pagan Christianity*, 233).

26. For example, Joe Boyd of Apex, a network of house churches, claims, "Now my church is the twelve friends I spend most of my time with; they are my missional and lifelong community. My pagan friends are church for me as well—while with them, I spend time with Jesus because he is with me. My community with these Las Vegas actors is just as strong as my Christian community, and I am slowly introducing Jesus to them." Quoted in Eddie Gibbs and Ryan Bolger, *Emerging Churches* (Grand Rapids: Zondervan, 2006), 248.

27. Jim Palmer, *Wide Open Spaces*, 39.

28. As argued by Cunningham, who writes that Jesus "did away with institutionalized religion and instead championed a real-life faith were he hung out with his followers in a way that was perhaps a bit reminiscent of Eden" (Cunningham, *Dear Church*, 165).

29. Gibbs and Bolger, *Emerging Churches*, back matter, 256.

30. Jones, *The New Christians*, 180.

31. Young, *The Shack*, 123.

32. Bavinck, *Reformed Dogmatics*, 413.

33. Cole, *Organic Church*, 135.

34. Timothy S. Laniak, *Shepherds After My Own Heart* (Downers Grove, Ill.: InterVarsity, 2006), 247.

35. Ibid.

36. One other note along these lines: The priesthood of all believers does not negate the need for authority structures in the church. The priesthood of all believers means, in part, that we all have equal access to God and are all given gifts to serve him. But mainly it is a reference to our holy standing before God. We must remember that Israel was called a kingdom of priests already in the Old Testament (Exod. 19:6) and yet only a few men could serve as literal priests! Our corporate holiness before God does not undermine the legitimacy of having different roles and differing levels of authority among God's people.

37. Meeks, *The First Urban Christians* (New Haven, Conn.: Yale Univ. Press, 1983), 111.

38. Bavinck, 305.

39. Ibid., 326.

40. Laniak, *Shepherds After My Own Heart*, 248.

41. Bonhoeffer, *Cost of Discipleship*, 281–82.

42. See Sanders, *Life After Church*, 62ff.

43. Barna, *Revolution*, 39.

44. Ibid., 129.

45. Gordon Fee, *The First Epistle to the Corinthians*, New International Commentary of the New Testament (Grand Rapids: Eerdmans, 1987), 537.

46. The pattern of weekly worship services rooted in the Jewish synagogue transferred easily into the New Testament church and carried right on through to the centuries that followed. Justin Martyr's description of a second century worship service is more or less what Christians have come to expect when they come to church: "On the day which is called Sunday, all who live in the cities or in the countryside gather together in one place. And the memoirs of the apostles or the writings of the prophets are read as long as there is time. Then, when the reader has finished, the president, in a discourse, admonishes and invites the people to practice these examples of virtue. Then we all stand up together and offer prayers. And, as we mentioned before, when we have finished the prayer, bread is presented, and wine with the water; the president likewise offers up prayers and thanksgivings according to his ability,

and the people assent by saying, Amen"; in The *First Apology of Justin Martyr* in *Liturgies of the Western Church*, Bard Thompson, comp. (New York: Meridian, 1961), 9.

47. Wolfgang Simson, *Emmanual Research Review*, issue No. 37, April 2008.

48. Viola and Barna, *Pagan Christianity*, 86.

49. Cunningham, *Dear Church*, 99–100.

50. For more on contemporary objections to preaching and my response to these objections, see Kevin DeYoung and Ted Kluck, *Why We're Not Emergent* (Chicago: Moody, 2008), 155–60.

51. John Stott, *Between Two Worlds: The Art of Preaching in the Twentieth Century* (Grand Rapids: Eerdmans, 1982), 15.

52. Hughes Oliphant Old, *The Reading and Preaching of the Scriptures in the Worship of the Christian Church*, vol. 1 (Grand Rapids: Eerdmans, 1998), 256.

53. Ibid., 93ff.

54. Ibid., 20.

55. Ibid., 234. Stott makes the same point in *Between Two Worlds*, 60–61.

56. Ibid., 264.

57. Sadly, some who think they hate preaching are actually dissatisfied because deep down, without their knowing it, they long to hear real preaching for the first time.

58. Timothy Keller, *The Reason for God* (New York: Dutton, 2008), 58ff. Elsewhere in the book, Keller defines religion as "a set of beliefs that explain what life is all about, who we are, and the most important things that human beings should spend their time doing" (15).

59. Rick James, *Jesus Without Religion* (Downers Grove, Ill.: InterVarsity, 2007).

60. E.g., "Who said anything about being a Christian? I'm not a Christian. . . . Those who love me come from every system that exists. . . . I have no desire to make them Christian, but I do want to join them in their transformation into sons and daughters of my Papa, into my brothers and sisters, into my Beloved" (Young, *The Shack*, 182). Similarly, Palmer writes, "I must tell you, I am not a proponent of "religion," even the "Christian" kind, but have never gone wrong following Jesus" (Palmer, *Divine Nobodies*, xxv).

61. Young, *The Shack*, 197–98.

62. Sweet, *The Gospel According to Starbucks* (Colorado Springs: Waterbrook, 2007), 111.

63. House Church guru Wolfgang Simson argues this point in *Emmanual Research Review*, Issue 37, April 2008.

64. Ibid.

65. "Learning from the House Church Movement in China," *CONTACT*, Summer 2008, 9.

66. Ibid., 10.

67. Ibid., 11.

68. Ibid.

69. Ibid., 10.

My father has received a good, balanced university education. . . . He has a master's degree, which means he's been forced fed so much information that he never wants to read another book in his life. You lose your curiosity.

– Iggy Pop, rock star

"Jake, you get wise. You get to church."

Cab Calloway (as Curtis), *The Blues Brothers* (1980)

Anyone who loves the dream of community more than the Christian community itself [warts and all] becomes a destroyer of the latter even though the devotion to the former is faultless and the intentions may be ever so honest, earnest and sacrificial.

– Dietrich Bonhoeffer, *Life Together*

CHAPTER 8

THE YEAR OF JUBILEE: HOW I LEARNED TO STOP WORRYING AND LOVE THE CHURCH

A t least twice a year we sit around our living room with our small group, with whatever book we're reading at the moment resting on our laps, and whine about how busy we are, and how little time we have for Bible reading and prayer.

"I'm just so busy with work." Heads nod. Affirmation all around.

"It's so hard with the kids. They're up so early." More heads nod.

We realize that nobody has done the reading for tonight, or if the reading was done, it was done in the car on the way over. We're all wiped out. Kevin and I just got off the road. Anthony's wife, Adrienne, has final exams coming up. The Newmans have a houseful of squirrelly kids. Let's just have another cup of coffee and catch up.

Imagine something with me for a moment. Imagine a year without itineraries. Imagine a year without business deadlines or taking work home with you; of conflicting soccer or Little League practices and schedules that eat up your weekend. No one-thousand-page reading list for your day or evening class as you balance school assignments and the day job.

Your vision of blessed relief probably differs from mine. This, friends, is my vision for the year of jubilee[1]: No Christian conferences, no Christian books written, bought, or published. Just Bible reading, prayer, and church attendance. No more reading about doing community. No more incubation-for-social-change meetings, and to be fair, no more book discussion groups. Reading. Praying. Church.

This is one of those chapters that in true revolutionary fashion may sound a little more implausibly, fetchingly "out there" than is truly possible. That's okay. You may also wonder why someone who makes a chunk of his living writing Christian books would suggest a year without buying, selling, or marketing books or materials of any kind. I don't really know either, except to say that I'm kind of sick of all of this stuff and in true Iggy Pop fashion am ready to sabotage my career.

What I'm proposing may be stunning in its utter simplicity. For one year, dedicate yourselves to the following: prayer, Bible reading, and involvement in a local church body.

Some of you may need to visit the Hazelden Clinic or some other such facility to clear your twitchy, needy, addiction to Christian books and resources. That's okay. There's probably a twelve-step program out there for you. Ironically, some well-meaning Christian has probably written a book on it.

You can use the time that you normally spend on those keeping-busy tasks doing something else, like spending time with your family or getting to know people at your church. And instead of reading the fifty-five books on your Amazon list, or on your virtual bookshelf, or on your real bookshelf, you'll read one.

Know, too, that I'm in the same boat. I have a shelfful of books that are dying to be read, partly because somewhere along the line I paid for them and now feel obligated to actually consume them. There are blogs on my feed that I'm woefully behind on. CDs that have been bought and not listened to. This all stresses me out. But this is me sabotaging my career.

ONE SUNDAY MORNING AT CHURCH

Having survived the congregational prayer, the multiple pregnancy announcements, and the bilingual worship, my wife and I settle into our yellow plastic chairs for another sermon. We've got Tristan with us this morning, and in true kid-in-church fashion he is engrossed in a coloring book, but he's also psyched because he helped us set up the three hundred or so chairs last night in the sanctuary. Even that process was a little peek behind the curtain. We arrived on Saturday evening, and arranged the moveable chairs into neat rows. We laid a Bible and hymnal on every seat, facing forward. Microphone stands were set up. The pulpit was arranged in front. We were there because my wife works a few hours a week at the church, cleaning and setting up for Sunday services, and Tristan and I decided to join her.

As it turns out, the other janitor brought his wife, and what was going to be another couple of humdrum hours of work became an impromptu gathering. We worked hard. We laughed. We talked about a variety of things both spiritual and banal. At the end I was tired and thankful for my church. I was thankful that Tristan got to help. Thankful that we have a Bible for every seat, and thankful that people work hard to make this happen each week.

It occurs to me that sometimes you do the thing (going to church) and then the feelings happen later. However, my generation seems to want the great feelings about church to come on the front end, so that one feels great each and every time one darkens the door of one's church. This strikes me as more than a little unrealistic.

This Sunday's sermon is from 2 Corinthians 5:11–15, which begins, "Since, then, we know what it is to fear the Lord, we try to persuade men" (NIV).

"Our church doesn't exist to give you ten ways to deal with stress, or to help you become a better person," Pastor Kevin says from the pulpit. "We're here to persuade you. We're here to preach to you."

This, partly, comes from knowing what it is to fear the Lord. Currently, if publishing trends are any indication, we serve a Lord who is our friend, our camping buddy, someone with whom we have intimacy, etc.

WHY I LOVE MY CHURCH

The message and the people around me listening, remind me of some things that I really appreciate about our church:

- **Propositions.** I'm glad I know, explicitly, what our church believes and affirms. These propositions manifest themselves not only as a statement of faith on a page, or a curriculum in a new members class, but in the lives of our congregants. I can look around the room and see an implicit understanding of God's sovereignty at work in the lives of the people I worship with, and that is a profound encouragement.

- **Sincerity.** Do I love singing "Santo, Santo, Santo"? Admittedly, no. But I do love the fact that our praise team is full of random people who fit into different demographics but share a passion for worshiping God through song. Even if I don't always "like" the songs, I love the sincerity with which they're sung, and that helps me worship.

- ***Our small group.*** Looking around the room, I can see Anthony and his wife, Adrienne, who is from Hungary. Because Anthony is an artist and thinks on a different wavelength than I do, I only understand about a third of what he's saying at a given moment, which doesn't matter because we still really like each other. Nathan, the bearded mathematician, always sits behind us. Nathan builds kites, cooks French cuisine, and has a sauna at his house (read: we have nothing in common), which I've visited and had great conversations in several times. I'm confident that we would know nothing of each other were it not for this small group, and by extension, our church's small-group ministry.

- ***Jarmo, Vandermolen, J.R., and his wife, Linzo.*** These are four college students we've gotten to know because they also go to our church, and because my wife mentors Linzo, which really means we just hang out a lot because we really like each other. Jarmo, Vandermolen, and J.R. are all guy friends of Linzo who got to know me because we all love professional wrestling. (Feel free to stop reading here, if that's too much for you.)

- ***Regner.*** Regner is a filmmaker buddy of mine who I met at a young-couples mixer at the home of the previous pastor of our church. Were it not for the church, and perhaps for Tom organizing said mixer, Regner and I may have never met, become friends, made a film together, been in a small group together, and started a fantasy football league together.

- ***Mentoring.*** We probably have too much mentoring at our church. Like most places, the popular kids at our church have adults lining up to mentor them, and there are kids who, it seems, now can't decide where to take a girl for coffee without asking their panel of mentors. Mentoring is a very positive, intentional part of life in our congregation. It is organized religion—the intentional seeking out of college students with the intention of mentoring them spiritually—but it often results in rich, lifelong friendships and growth on the part of both mentor and mentee.

• ***Structure, elders, and deacons.*** Our elders come in all shapes and sizes. Being a Reformed church in Michigan, there is the requisite eight-foot-tall Dutchman, but there is also a bald schoolteacher, a guy who works in the warehouse at a local dairy, a PhD, and a shoe repairman. I've had conversations with all of these guys, and consider all of them my friends. I also know the depth of their commitment to Christ and to leading our church. I thank God for this. I'm glad there's a process in place for choosing these men, as laid out in great detail in 1 Timothy 3.

    I never appreciated these men more than during the two-year period between the retirement of our first pastor, and the arrival of Kevin. I realized then that our church belonged to God, and was not simply a reflection of the guy behind the pulpit.

    "Obey your leaders and submit to them," Scripture says, "for they are keeping watch over your souls, as those who will have to give an account. Let them do this with joy and not with groaning, for that would be of no advantage to you" (Heb. 13:17). I'm glad our leaders perform this service with joy and are not, as Barna suggests, among that percentage of Americans "deriving all their spiritual input (and output) through the Internet."

• ***Our lack of happy endings.*** Perhaps this is what author/speaker/futurist types mean when they talk/write about being "real." As I look around the room this morning, I see a great man with Lou Gehrig's disease, holding hands with his sweet wife. I see another couple, the husband just diagnosed with cancer that will probably take his life in six months or so. I see a weird military vet guy who fried his brain on drugs in Iraq, and who we follow out to the lobby when he goes to the bathroom because we're afraid for the safety of our kids. I see my father-in-law who has a degenerative brain disease that has destroyed his intellect and his ability to communicate and will take his life before it's all said and done.

As evangelicals we've become addicted to "happy ending" stories where we go through "x" (hard thing) and then start praying and then—Shazam!—God makes everything better and we have a nice, utopian story to tell where we are the hero who ends up with the great job, the great family, the time off, the free plane ticket, the lost purse, or the great healthy kids. The fact of the matter is, sometimes (often)

> **SOMETIMES (OFTEN) THE HAPPY ENDING IS HEAVEN, AND THE GETTING THERE IS THE FORMATIVE PART OF OUR SANCTIFICATION.**

the happy ending is heaven, and the getting there is a really difficult but formative part of our sanctification. And sometimes what God wants in the interim is for us to find our happiness, holiness, and identity in Him, rather than our perfect jobs, perfect 2.5 kids (or 6.5 kids in the case of our church), and perfect testimonies.

- *Community (Love).* I am sick of books about community, so I'm hesitant to write about it in this space. I've learned that community rarely feels like that mountaintop experience in college, in the dorms, at midnight, when you and your buddies are confessing your sins, talking about girls, and perhaps talking about God and solving the church's problems over cold pizza. That situation is tailor-made for community because you're all the same, and you're all stuck there with nothing else to do. It's easy to love your friends in college because they're all basically

193

like you. Community becomes much harder when there's something on the line—like my time, my money, my ideals, my precious opinions, my ego, and my privacy.

That said, community is people arranging to pay each others' bills when times get tough. It means arranging to grocery shop for someone when that someone suddenly has to be the primary caregiver to their sick spouse all day. It means spending time with your disabled family member or friend who is rapidly declining in health, when that time isn't fun, rewarding, or especially productive. And it's about those friends staying friends with us through our cynicism and sometimes bitterness.

- *Preaching.* I can't read Paul's letters to Timothy and Titus without thinking that preaching is really important. Preaching is more than a conversation, or a collection of inspirational thoughts to ponder. It's a passionate, desperate plea for life through the gospel, as Paul declared to Timothy: "In the presence of God and of Christ Jesus, who will judge the living and the dead, and in view of his appearing and his kingdom, I give you this charge: Preach the Word; be prepared in season and out of season; correct, rebuke, and encourage—with great patience and careful instruction" (2 Timothy 4:1–2 NIV).

As he continues to preach through the 2 Corinthians 5 text, Kevin asks the question: What is the motivation for my ministry? Paul's motives, according to verses 11 and 14 were both the fear of the Lord and the love of Christ. We need to know Christ as both a judge and Savior.

THE FEAR FOLKS AND THE LOVE PEOPLE

The fear folks are probably the people for whom books like *Revolution*, *Wide Open Spaces*, and *Starbucks* were written. We have some of them in our denomination; people who are so busy pounding their fists about the fear of the Lord that they also forget that God is love.

"It's quite possible that you put on this mask of the fear of the Lord, but you're just a jerk," Kevin suggests. "You just don't like people. It's possible."

The love people, likewise, have their own blinders on. There are the Christians who ignore Christ the judge. He's not here to be judgmental, they suggest. Rather, He's here to be your intimate friend and ministry partner. To the love people, God wants to be in a relationship with you, and He loves everyone, equally, in the same way.

"You look at Scripture," Kevin suggests, "and getting close to the living God is a fearful thing."

Paul's motivation in his letter to the Corinthians was to get them to see that God was both entirely loving and kind, and also entirely the object of fear. Both of these ideas are necessary if one is to truly understand and worship this God we say we believe in. We can't understand love without also understanding that the penalty Christ paid on the cross—penal substitutionary atonement for our total depravity—was the most loving act ever committed in the history of man. It was an act far more loving than those portrayed in the usual smattering of "buddy Jesus" or "intimacy with God" books where Jesus is your therapist and there you lie on His cosmic chaise lounge, waiting for Him to dispense beauty and/or easy solutions until the last grain of sand runs out of the hourglass and your time is up.

The gospel is a simple invitation to believe in who Jesus is and what He has done to bring us to God. As stated by J. C. Ryle in his 1879 book, *Holiness*:

> But I do bid you come to Christ and be saved. The day of decision
> must come sometime. Why not this very hour? Why not today, while
> it is called today? Why not this very night, ere the sun rises tomor-

row morning? Come to him who died for sinners on the cross, and invites all sinners to come to him by faith and be saved. Come to my Master, Jesus Christ. . . . Mercy is ready for you. Christ is ready to receive you. Christ will receive you gladly, and welcome you among his children.[2]

GO

If I could leave you with one thought, it's this: Go. Go to church. Don't go for the coffee, the presentations, the music, or the amenities. Don't even go for the feelings you may or may not get when you go because, no offense, these feelings may or may not be trustworthy most of the time. Go for the gospel. Go for the preaching. Go to be near to God's Word.

Around me I see our cinder-block sanctuary, green carpet, yellow chairs, and a good friend in the pulpit, preaching the gospel. I see other good friends and their families scattered throughout the room. I will see them next week, and the week after that, Lord willing. It strikes me that people will go to great lengths to find God—Jim Palmer quit church, George Barna started a "Revolution," and Leonard Sweet went to Starbucks. But here, in our sanctuary, I'm given the privilege and gift of learning about God in all of His attributes or as Jonathan Edwards puts it, His "diverse excellencies." And His excellencies manifest themselves in these people, in our preaching, in our friendships, in our community and fellowship together.

There are many people leaving the church, and supposedly finding God. But I found Him here, and by His grace, I'll keep finding Him here. I love my church.

NOTE

1. The people of Israel knew how to throw a jubilee, a great time of rest given them by God. For Israel, the year of jubilee was a year off from sowing the land and gathering the crops (Leviticus 25:8–12), a holy time devoted to honoring God and your fellow man (verses 13–18).
2. J. C. Ryle, *Holiness* (Peabody, Mass.: Hendrickson, 2007), 284.

Strive to live a courageous life. Confess

Christ before men. Whatever station you

occupy, in that station confess Christ. . . .

Strive to live a joyful life. Live like men who

look for that blessed hope—the second

coming of Jesus Christ.

J.C. Ryle, *Holiness*

But as for you, O man of God, flee these things.

Pursue righteousness, godliness, faith, love,

steadfastness, gentleness. Fight the good fight of

the faith. Take hold of the eternal life to which you

were called and about which you made the good

confession in the presence of many witnesses.

1 Timothy 6:11–12

DEAR TRISTAN:

TO MY SON REGARDING MY HOPES AND DREAMS FOR HIM AS THEY PERTAIN TO THE CHURCH

Dear Tristan,

By the time you read this, it might be hip to like church again. Right now it isn't, but luckily for us, you're five, and for you church is just another place with good toys, friends, and lots of space to run.

You love church now, and you love it for many of the same reasons we love it. You get to see your friends there every week, and you know they're going to be there, because their parents (and we) have committed to being there. You get Goldfish crackers and juice there, while we get doughnuts and bad coffee, but the idea is the same. Friendships and relationships. You're getting to know people whom you'll hopefully know for a long time because you share a bond in Christ.

There may very well be times in your life when you wonder why we're making you go to church. And let me say now that we won't be doing it to make your life more difficult, or because we want to be "right" or "in charge." We'll be doing it because we love church ourselves, we want to honor God by worshiping Him with other believers, and we care about your spiritual growth. And let me also say that when you get to be my age, you'll understand. I understand now why Mimi and Poppy made me go to church all those years, and I'm so glad they did.

There may very well be a long period in your life when you have an indifferent or maybe even hostile relationship with church. As I look back, the majority of my grade school years were spent in church drawing cars and football players. I wish I could have those Sundays back, but to be honest I'm not sure what I would do with them. I was probably indifferent, but I still got to sit through a lot of sermons, hear a lot of Scripture, and sing a lot of hymns—many of which I remember to this day and have sung in my head while being wheeled into surgery, led into a boxing ring for sparring, or putting my hand in the Astroturf in front of about six hundred pounds of ex-convict defensive linemen. There's Scripture and comfort in those hymns. I sang them in a cold flat in Ukraine when I wasn't sure we'd be able to take you home and I hurt more inside than I'd ever hurt in my life.

In my early twenties I visited churches that looked more like megamalls than sanctuaries, and met people who seemed more concerned with looking hot while stepping out of their Jaguars than worshiping God or caring about people in need. If you ever find yourself in a church situation like this, I would encourage you to visit some other churches. They're not all glorified country clubs like this. In my late twenties and early thirties I seem to be encountering just as many people who are so in tune with their own hurts, and so intent on critiquing the church that some of them are writing whole books about the subject.

There may come a day when you look around your church and don't see very many people who look like you. Perhaps they're all married and you're not. They may all have big families and you don't. You may think nobody in church votes like you do, or thinks like you do. I encourage you to ask questions of these people. Get to know them. Ask them why they're still in church after all of these years and listen carefully to their answers. I would bet that very few of them will say things like "obligation" or "because it's a vibrant discussion" or "to ask questions" or "because we've always done it." People don't give up large portions of their lives for questions. People make counterintuitive decisions—like going to church—for truth and for a faith that they'll take to the grave.

I pray that one day you'll be able to ask your pastor about free will versus predestination. I hope you'll ask him about the Trinity. About infant versus believer's baptism. Not because these are things that divide, but because it will be evidence that you care about your faith and hold it dear. Nothing would make me happier, Son. I pray that one day you'll be able to articulate what it is that you believe, not because you'll want to use it to win arguments, but because you'll be passionate about sharing the good news of the gospel of Jesus Christ. And out of this good news I pray that God will use you some-how. I pray that you'll always be kind. That you'll have a heart for those less fortunate than you, and will always be moved by the struggles of others. I pray that you'll be bold in professing your faith before men.

I pray that you'll meet your friends in church. You know that I've met friends in a variety of crazy places—boxing gyms, football fields, bars, coffee shops, workplaces, etc.—but you can also tell that the majority of my real friends in life, the people who will be with me through good times and bad, come from church. These are the people who pray for us, and with whom we "do life." It's a privilege.

And along those lines, I want to tell you that church is more than the soap opera that your mom and I make it sometimes. Doing life with people isn't always pretty. People don't always agree and sometimes those disagreements can be unpleasant. You're not going to like everybody in your church. But my prayer for you, and for us, is that our shared commitment to Christ will overcome this too, and we'll grow in love and respect for everyone in our congregation.

I pray that one day you'll profess your love for a special girl in front of a church full of your friends and those you worship with. I pray that you'll commit, in front of these friends and God, to lead her spiritually, and that your young family will be a vibrant part of the body of Christ. Love her with all your heart, like I've tried to love your mom.

I pray that God would surround you with people who challenge you to die to yourself and your sins, and I pray that if I am that person at some point in your life, that our relationship would be strong enough to weather it.

And I pray that your relationship with your wife will look a lot like the one that Mimi and Poppy have had all these years. As I type this they've been married for thirty-eight years, and are still going strong and the church has played a huge role in their lives. They've changed churches a few times over the years, for various reasons, but they've always been committed to a body, and that commitment, I'm convinced, is one reason why they're still happily married. Marriages like theirs don't just happen in our culture.

I also hope that, at some point, you'll get a chance to experience the body of Christ through hard times. If there's one thing I've learned in my years of church involvement, it's that hard things happen to everybody. There's sin in this world, and as a result, our bodies are in a constant state of decay, and our lives are almost always, it seems, in turmoil. Nearly every family in our church has dealt with job losses, cancer, heart disease, marital discord, infertility, the death of a child, or a myriad of other tough circumstances. Through that, I've seen the body of Christ work in wonderful ways. I've seen people give sacrificially with their money and their time. I've been prayed with and prayed for. We've had Scripture show up in our mailbox every day for a month. I've had the privilege of trying to pray others through their hard times as well.

I've seen great men crippled by disease—these were men who were the picture of health, intellect, and athleticism in their healthy years. But worshiping with them in sickness, as their usefulness in this world wanes, is a privilege. Seeing them makes me proud of our church, and proud to know the Lord.

Church isn't a magic pill that you take, that punches your ticket for heaven. Nor is it a glorified social/country club you attend to be around people who talk/think/look/act like you do. It's a place to go each week to hear the Word of God spoken, taught, and affirmed. It's a place to sing praises to our God, even if those songs do sometimes feel a bit awkward. It's a place to serve others. It's a place to be challenged. Sometimes you'll feel uncomfortable with those challenges, because sometimes your life will need to change. This has been the case with me.

It's about more than fund-raising, or networking, or meeting a girl, or even great things like serving the poor and reaching out to the community. I hope you'll always know that the Christian life isn't about what you can do for God, but rather about what God did for you on the cross. If this message isn't central in your church, again, you may need to find a new one.

But for now, enjoy your toys. Enjoy your Sunday school classes, and I'll try to do something with the piles of paper you bring home from them each week. Enjoy your friends, and enjoy the knowledge you're acquiring about the Christ that you asked to live in your heart, who revealed Himself through

Scripture, and about whom we can know things. It's only through Christ that I can do even an adequate job as your father.

Love Always,

Dad

'Mid toil and tribulation,

And tumult of her war,

She waits the consummation

Of peace forevermore;

Till, with the vision glorious,

Her longing eyes are blest,

And the great Church victorious

Shall be the Church at rest.

"The Church's One Foundation" verse 5

TOWARD A THEOLOGY OF PLODDING VISIONARIES

The church in North America is suffering from a crisis in ecclesiology.[1] The crisis is most Christians don't have any ecclesiology. As much as people love to talk about community these days, very few practitioners have given serious thought to the doctrine of the church.[2] In fact, many of those writing about the church today are doing so to blast the church or express their rationale for leaving her institutional form altogether.

The church is often understood as nothing but a plural word for *Christian*, so that wherever two or three are gathered in Christ's name—regardless of where they are, what they are doing, and what sort of polity is in place (if any)—there you have a church. The cause and result of this minimalist definition of church is our current crisis in ecclesiology.

So what should be done to solve this crisis? Of course, part of the answer is to develop a more thoughtful, biblically robust, and historically rooted ecclesiology. This book has been an attempt to develop, in a pastorally sensitive and culturally savvy way, such a doctrine of the church. We've tried our best to lay out a faithful and captivating picture of the church as the Bible describes her and as she's lived out and lived into in real life. But renewed ecclesiology is only part of the answer. We need theological renewal in other areas as well.

It's impossible to say that one doctrine is most essential to the health and long-term vitality of the church. The church certainly needs a solid understanding of who Christ is and what is meant by the Trinity and what to make of the authority of the Bible and the nature of the gospel. All of these, and a dozen other doctrines, are essential to the well-being of the church. But one doctrine in particular must be recovered and more fully embraced if the North American church is to pull out of its current crisis in ecclesiology. The doctrine I'm thinking of, surprisingly enough, is the doctrine of original sin.

"IN ADAM'S FALL, WE SINNED ALL"

The doctrine of original sin teaches that every single human being who ever was, is, or shall be inherited from Adam a sinful nature that makes us predisposed to wickedness and rebellion against God. The Belgic Confession (1561) summarizes the doctrine this way: "We believe that by the disobedience of Adam original sin has been spread through the whole human race. It is a corruption of all nature—an inherited depravity which even infects small infants in their mother's womb, and the root which produces in man every sort of sin. It is therefore so vile and enormous in God's sight that it is enough to condemn the human race" (Article 15).

For most of church history—certainly from Augustine on down—most

Christians, especially the Reformers and their confessional and evangelical heirs, have believed in original sin. The rosy view of human nature espoused by Pelagius was condemned as heretical at the Council of Ephesus in 431. Since then, if there has been any shared starting point across the theological spectrum of Christianity it was this: We are born into the world with a bent toward evil and in need of a Savior.

More recently, however, prominent "evangelicals" have questioned the validity of the doctrine of original sin. One author mocks it, making original sin the subject of Mary's Magnificat until it sounds ridiculous.[3] Another denies it, claiming that "Jesus believed in original goodness."[4] Another rejects it, finding total depravity "biblically questionable, extreme, and profoundly unhelpful."[5] And yet another is completely fed up with it, basing his rejection of original sin on the belief that "Augustine's doctrine of depravity was based on a particular linguistic and cultural reading of certain passages of the Bible."[6]

It's worth mentioning at this point Alan Jacobs's reflection that those "who credit or blame Augustine for the 'invention' of original sin contend that he misread Paul; and it seems to me that the scholars who make that contention tend to be attached to the Christian faith in some way." In other words, Christians don't like to disagree straight up with Paul, so they try to sidestep the doctrine claiming that Augustine misinterpreted him. But as Jacobs points out, Tertullian, two hundred years prior to Augustine, saw "our participation in [Adam's] transgression, our fellowship in his death, our expulsion from Paradise." Tertullian believed that "the evil that exists in the soul . . . is antecedent, being derived from the fault of our origin and having become in a way natural to us." His contemporary, Cyprian of Carthage, spoke of a "primeval contagion" and the "wounds" we all receive from Adam.[7] So if Augustine misread Paul, he was not the first (and certainly not the last).

More important than the record of history is the testimony of Scripture. It's hard to see how the doctrine of inherited and total depravity is not taught in the pages of Scripture. No one is righteous (Rom. 3:10). "All have sinned and fall short of the glory of God" (Rom. 3:23). The human heart "is deceitful above all things, and desperately sick" (Jer. 17:9). The natural man is dead in trespasses and sin (Eph. 2:1). By nature, we "[pass] our days in malice and envy, hated by others and hating one another" (Titus 3:3). We are inclined toward evil (Gen. 6:5), conceived in sin, and "brought forth in iniquity" (Psalm 51:5). All of us "like sheep have gone astray" (Isa. 53:6). Even "our righteous acts are like filthy rags" before the Lord (Isa. 64:6 NIV). We are by nature not just morally tainted, but "children of wrath," deserving of God's punishment, even before we actually sin in our flesh (Eph. 2:3). Even on the best of days, we are divided, doing what we don't want to do and failing to do what we know is right (Rom. 7:18–19).

Because of the fall, we are hardwired toward evil. We sinned in Adam and died through his trespass, inheriting his guilt and a corrupt nature (see Rom. 5:12–21).

It's precisely this doctrine of original sin, and the related doctrines of total depravity and the divided self, that need to be recovered if we are to have a biblical, realistic, and Christ-centered doctrine of the church.

SINNING SAINTS AND SINNING SINNERS

For starters, the doctrine of original sin would go a long way toward understanding the church's imperfections—past, present, and future. It's not excuse, but it is an explanation: the church is full of sinners. We are, as Luther reminded us, *simul iustus et peccator*, "at the same time justified and sinner."

Likewise, the church is at the same time the bride of Christ and the Lord's harlot. Yes, it's true. The church always should look different from the world, but with so many millions of people in the church coming from so many different backgrounds and places in life, it's not surprising that every church has a truckload of issues to deal with. Our churches have pew after pew (and pulpit after pulpit) of selfish, proud, petty, lustful, greedy people. Many of them are trying to put to death the deeds of the flesh, but it is slow, hard, sometimes inconsistent work. And other churchgoers are simply unregenerate, sitting in church a couple of times a month out of custom or obligation. With such a mix of people—sinning saints and sinning sinners—in our congregations, it's no wonder that things can look pretty grim.

Some have told me, "The church is kind of like sausage—it's better to just enjoy the thing and not look to see how it all comes together behind the scenes." Maybe that's why I haven't gotten disillusioned, at least not yet. In less than a decade in ministry, I've seen pastors getting divorced, pastors addicted to alcohol, pastors addicted to prescription drugs, pastors burned out, staff conflict, church factions, silly fights over music stands and music styles, lazy Christians, hypocritical Christians, adulterous Christians, power plays, power struggles, insincerity, insecurity, and a hundred other legitimate knocks on the church. I've been hurt in the church, and I'm naive if I don't think that I've hurt people in the church.

This is sad and not how it should be. But "not how it should be" is not the same as "not how it is going to be." Certainly, some churches are better and healthier than others. The goal is to grow in godliness. But the church will be full of sin so long as she is full of sinners—which is kind of the point I thought. It's more than a little ironic that the same folks who want the church to ditch the phoney, plastic persona and become a haven for broken, imperfect sinners are ready to leave the church when she is broken, imperfect, and sinful.

Partly to blame for this impatience is the idealized view "the church is lame" crowd has of the early church. According to one leader in the simple house-church movement, "The Early Church was unstoppable until in A.D. 324, when the movement turned into a monument once the first church building was erected."[8] Another author claims that "during its first 150 years, the Christian church had not even heard of church buildings. In those days the church was a mobile, flexible, relational, humble, inclusive reality that spread like wildfire."[9] Or again: "The New Testament church had no buildings, it had no clergy, it had no money, and it had no authority. People relied on each other. . . . People met in other people's houses. No neutral, cold, impersonal buildings, but somebody's private living space. . . . Decisions were made as a community and life was lived in the context of community. And the community of believers crossed the divides of social and economic status. So what went wrong? All this changed with Constantine."[10]

Not only does it strain credulity past the breaking point to think that buildings caused the wheels to fall off the unstoppable church bus, it's also unhelpfully idealistic. No wonder so many people are disillusioned with the church today. They think it was nigh unto perfect back in the good old days. And then came institutionalism, or Constantine, or Christendom, or Greek thinking, or the Enlightenment, or modernism, or systematic theology, or Old Princeton, or whatever your boogeyman looks like. The church used to be a rockin,' sweet place, and then, bam!, it all fell apart, and now we are finally enlightened enough to start picking up the pieces.

We need a little more realism. I praise God for the apostles and prophets, for the first apologists and evangelists, for the holy army of martyrs whose blood became the seed of the church. But untainted and pristine they were not. The New Testament church was not always "a church of power and sincere community," and it certainly wasn't a "beatific vision."[11] The early church had heretics and divisions and controversies and sexual immorality and power struggles and money issues and authority issues and marriage problems and just about anything else you can think of. You'd think we had never read 1 Corinthians before.

The early church was remarkable in many ways. I would never claim to have the courage of Peter or the love of John or the fortitude of Paul or the peace of Polycarp or the intellect of Tertullian. But the church always struggled. She grew in those first centuries, to be sure, but more

> **THE EARLY CHURCH HAD HERETICS AND DIVISIONS AND CONTROVERSIES AND SEXUAL IMMORALITY AND POWER STRUGGLES.**

slowly than we sometimes think. The church did not so much explode on the scene as she grew very steadily over several centuries.[12] The evangelism of the countryside took more than one thousand years.[13] And even when the church was growing, it did so in fits and starts, with heroes and heretics, with bad guys and boring times, and quiet faithfulness and slow-bearing fruit. Saints and sinners we are and have always been.

WITH GOD ALL THINGS ARE POSSIBLE, BUT SOME THINGS DON'T COME UNTIL LATER

If the doctrine of original sin can give us a more accurate view of our own history, it can also give us a more realistic appraisal of the world's future. I am not averse to taking risks or dreaming big dreams. In fact, I am often challenging our church to have a vision bigger than we know how to fulfill. I like the gumption of those who attempt great things for God and expect great things from God (to use William Carey's familiar phrase). But the dreams of many church-leavers and church-bashers are of the utopian kind.[14] And world history is littered with the remains of those who were crushed—emotionally and sometimes literally—by the weight of heaven-on-earth fantasies.

I believe in heaven. I even believe, as I've heard a thousand times in the past couple years, that heaven is coming to us, that this earth will be renewed. But we are not there yet. And heaven won't come without some pretty major and noticeable events happening first, like . . . the cataclysmic destruction of the cosmos and the return of Jesus Christ. So even if everything must change, everything will not change. As long as there are sinners on the earth, and a whole bunch of them unregenerate ones at that, and as long as we labor under the curse, and as long as the earth continues to groan in the pains of childbirth, the world is not going to be one happy planet of shalom and sharing.

WE NEED TO GUARD AGAINST IDEALISM THAT FIGURES HEAVEN ON EARTH IS POSSIBLE WITH A LITTLE BIT OF LOVE.

I really want to be careful here that this doesn't come across as an apologetic for the status quo. One of the reasons activist types don't like the doctrine of original sin is because they fear that people will not attempt what should be changed if they believe it is not in their power to create real change.[15] We need to be reminded that there are problems we can solve, or at least make better. With hard work, wisdom, and lots of God's grace, the lot in life for millions can improve for the good. But we also need to guard against utopian idealism—an idealism that figures heaven on earth is possible with a little bit of love and assumes that anyone can follow the way of Jesus without the requisite change of heart, without being born again. This kind of idealism explains why the missional/community transformation/global revolutionary folks reject or ignore the doctrine of original sin. It doesn't fit with their vision of a fair and just planet. And it doesn't fit with their hope that people everywhere will lay down their weapons and start loving each other like Jesus.[16]

The fact of the matter is we are not going to "transform the face of planet Earth to a place of justice, peace and equity, a place without suffering."[17] It's no coincidence that disillusionment is such a big theme in the church-leaving literature. Many of these passionate, well-intentioned youngish church-leavers have a vision for the world that is so unlike anything promised on this side of heaven that they can't help but feel disappointed and angry with the church for not getting the world where they think it can go.

For example, one church-leaver imagines a world transformed by one hundred thousand Mother Teresas and one hundred thousand Bonos. In such a world, we wouldn't need government because we would govern ourselves, or borders or dividing lines because every nation would get along with all the others, or the military because we would have no enemies, or police because we would all serve and protect each other. We would need no money because we would all give to those in need; no hospitals or doctors or mental institutions because disease, this church-leaver writes, is often linked to a lack of love; and no nursing homes because we would care for the elderly in our homes. Such a utopian place is possible if only we acted like the "little Christs" we are supposed to be. It is to the church's shame, therefore, that "very few people are capable of envisioning a redeemed world except rock stars."[18]

Another church-leaver imagines a world where parents always love each other and kids are always honored; where friendships are never weighed down and everyone is ready to give and serve; where needy people never go uncared for and trust is the basic assumption in every relationship; where bosses are wonderful and you rarely wait in lines; where fast-food restaurants go out of business because all the food is cooked with care and no one eats alone; where there is health inside and out; where all remaining misunderstandings and problems are handled with grace, fairness, and love. This is the kingdom of God one church-leaver hopes for in our congregations, communities, and cities.[19]

This is a wonderful dream (except for those employed at McDonalds and Burger King), but it sounds more like the new heavens and new earth of Revelation 21–22 and not like the world that will have wars and rumors of wars right till the very end (see Matthew 24:6). And actually, the typical dream for the kingdom of God that is proposed today looks unlike the vision of Revelation in one important way: There's very little mention of the King. Emergents, church-leavers, and the missional folks have a vision for a planet without mourning, crying, or pain (Rev. 21:4). But they don't talk much about the Alpha and Omega offering the water of life there (21:6), or the fulfillment of the covenant promise that God will be our God and we will be His people (21:3, 7). We don't hear about a vision of a renewed earth that is not only free from suffering, but dazzling in its purity and holiness (21:9–21), and free from everything and everyone that is unclean (21:8, 27). Worst of all, in all the utopian dreams of the kingdom here on earth, we hear little about worshiping God and the Lamb (22:3), almost nothing about the best news of all that God will be with us as our God (21:3); He will be our light and we will reign forever and ever (22:5). This is the dream of everyone living in Christ-centered reality.

A MATTER OF PERSPECTIVE

The doctrine of original sin can also help the church from drifting away from what matters most. The danger of incessant polling and trend watching is that the church's target will always be changing. We will be forever doomed to chase relevance, manage people's perceptions of the church, and catch up with cutting edge. The nice thing about the doctrine of original sin is that it focuses our attention on issues that are a little more timeless. People will always be sinners. So our main problem is not lack of integration or balance, or lack of success or education, or even poverty and injustice, as serious as these problems can be. Our main problem will always be sin. And, hence, we are always in need of a Savior. This doesn't mean we can be blissfully ignorant of the world around us, but it means our focus will be squarely on the gospel. We can forget about being the church of what's happening now, and relearn to be the church of Christ, and Him crucified.

One of my criticisms of the evangelical church is that every decade or so a new round of voices emerge to tell us that the church is about to implode and there will be no Christian presence left for our children unless we change everything, like, right now. I'm not old enough to recall many of the fads that have come and gone. But I do remember when seeker-sensitive churches were all the rage and a contemporary worship style would supposedly solve everything. So we plugged in the guitars, turned up the lights, and made the sermons more practical. Trinity Church became Apple Blossom Community Church, and First Lutheran became Celebration of Life Church. Today, missional is all the rage and we're told that a little more attention to Starbucks culture will supposedly fix what ails the church. We've plugged into liturgy, turned down the lights, and made the sermons more dialogical. Christ Church has become The Journey and First Baptist now holds a 10:03 Fusion gathering. This too shall pass.

According to George Barna, "The window of opportunity for reaching Americans with the gospel appears to be closing rapidly." The fascinating thing is Barna wrote this back in 1990.[20] The window must almost be shut by now. If the Christian community was in 1990 already "losing the battle"[21] and the forecast for the decade was "mostly cloudy,"[22] surely the church must be about ready to throw in the towel on the edge of the 2010s. For Barna, the church always seems to be failing, which in turn always necessitates doing

217

church differently, or in the case of *Revolution*, the latest Barna offering, not doing church at all.

But for the life of me I can't figure out why so many evangelicals get their knickers in a twist over the latest trends. We need a little perspective. What's hot and new now will, unless it is the rediscovery of something old and biblical, end up being embarrassingly out of date and unhelpful in just a few years. For example, in his "classic" *Frog in the Kettle*, Barna argued that responding to "felt needs through highly personalized messages" was the answer to declining attendance figures.[23] Now hardly anyone talks of felt needs and personalized messages. This kind of preaching is seen as stale, recycled self-help psychology, and out of touch. The services in 1990 were supposed "to shed existing attitudes of piety and [solemnness], in favor of attitudes of anticipation, joy and fulfillment."[24] Such a service would seem inauthentic by today's standards. Now the worship service is supposed to be in touch with the raw, authentic pain of our doubting selves. Among the achievable goals for the 1990s were "restoring self-esteem" and "championing Christian morals" by making the legislative, judicial, and administrative ends of our government responsive to a higher order of thoughts.[25] Today, admitting our dysfunctions is the thing to do and few things are more lampooned by the cutting-edge missional folks more than attempts on the Religious Right to legislate our morality. In 1990, Barna argued that "whatever barriers and difficulties may face the Church today, having enough local churches is not the issue."[26] He figured (incorrectly) that there would be a net gain of fifty thousand churches in the 1990s. Today, there is hardly a church executive out there who isn't making the case for more churches and hardly a denomination of any stripe that doesn't consider church planting one of its top priorities.

I don't mean to pick on Barna, but because he has often written about how the church needs to change, he provides a nice test case. And very often, his descriptions of the present and prescriptions for the future do not pass the test. The 1990s were supposed to be "a time in which the Church will either explode with new growth or quietly fade into a colorless thread

> **THINGS ARE NOT THE WORST THEY'VE EVER BEEN. THE END OF THE CHURCH IN AMERICA IS NOT NIGH.**

in the fabric of secular culture."[27] Wrong and wrong. The church did not explode in growth and it did not fade into oblivion. By conservative estimates, there were 52 million people in church on the weekends back in 1990 and there were 52 million in church each week in 2005 (see chapter 1).

This book is not meant to be an apology for nothing but more of the same; rather, it's a plea for realism. Things are not the worst they've ever been. The end of the church in America is not nigh upon us. There are grave failings in the church, in the evangelical church as much as anywhere. We need better preaching, better theology, more love for Jesus, more involvement in our neighborhoods, more evangelism, more crosscultural missions, more generosity, more biblical literacy, less worldliness, less trend-tracing, and better discipleship. The church in this country will always have something—many things—to work on. But in the midst of our struggles, we need to guard against wild hyperbole. We need to exercise more caution before we pronounce the end of the church as we know it. We need a little more humility before we announce everything must change. And we need a little more wisdom before we reinvent the church for yet another time—let alone before we pitch her to the curb altogether.

A LOOK IN THE MIRROR

Finally, the doctrine of original sin forces us to take a more honest look at ourselves and our remaining indwelling sin. This goes for all of us—church-lovers and church-leavers.

It includes pastors too. Pastors need to own up to their control issues and fear of man. We need to admit that the problem isn't always out there. We have not always represented Christ well. We have not always loved the flock or cared a jot or tittle about the world around us. Sometimes our sermons are formulaic and dreadfully dull.

Churchgoers need to admit that they don't always look much like Christ. Many of them need to own some responsibility for the negative impression people have of the church. Others need to see that they live in a wacky Christian subculture that, for all its blessings, looks strange to outsiders. Churches need to realize they have often been more adept at welcoming clean-cut, suburban families than pierced, indie-rocker, artist types. The church needs to follow up with those who leave and be patient and humble enough to hear their complaints, whether they prove to be justified or not.

And the disgruntled "church stinks" crowd needs to be careful that their disillusionment does not become an idol, that they do not find their identity in being jaded.[28] I encourage any Disgruntled Johnny reading this book to ask yourself, "What am I *not* disgruntled about?" Do you really want to always be the "nobody understands me," too-cool-for-school guy (or gal)? To always be the "Thomas Kinkade is a disgrace to art, church people are lame, sermons are so stupid" kind of cynic is not good for the soul. So what if people in the church have never heard of *Akeelah and the Bee* (Leonard Sweet says you must be living under a rock if you haven't), watch *Facing the Giants*, and listen to "family friendly" radio stations. Sure, a lot of the Christian pop culture stuff is pretty cheesy; it's certainly not gritty or raw. Fine. Don't like it. I often don't. But a lot of the other stuff out there is pretty vile. Maybe churchgoers would stop harping on the young people to listen to Smile FM around the clock if the cultural hipsters stopped congratulating themselves for liking Eminem and his manufactured authenticity, as if being real about life is an excuse for being perverse. Maybe churchgoers can learn to overlook some strange tattoos and hair configurations if their counterparts will learn that swearing, drinking alcohol, and doing whatever else seems fetchingly rebellious and oh-so-not suburban middle class are not the leading indicators of spiritual maturity. Maybe the churchgoers will have the eyes to see what needs to change in the institutional church, and the church-leavers will recognize that skipping church to go golfing or walk in the woods does not make you a real revolutionary.

And in our hypertherapeutic culture, we all need to realize that sometimes being in touch with our pain and being real about our doubts and authentic about our struggles is a form of narcissism and self-absorption more than maturity. We could all use a little less complaining and a little more gratitude. It's easy to blast the church for all its failures. It's harder to live in it day after day, year after year, with all its ho-hum humdrum and slowly, consistently make a difference.

I know the problems of my church as well as anyone. We have goals that include supporting more missionaries, doing better at evangelism and mercy ministry, and adding more small groups. Our church is not exceptional. We do some things pretty well. We do other things poorly. But we bring meals to single moms, talk to homeless people who come in and help them get a meal if they need it, write checks when folks lose their job, go pray at the hospital with people, and share life together.

With all the ugly sausage making I've seen in the church, I've also witnessed incredible sacrifice and generosity. I've marveled a number of times at why all these people voluntarily show up for worship on Sunday, give of their time and money, and commit to loving those who are or once were complete strangers. I've overhead plenty of newcomers being invited over for dinner. I've been moved to tears as people tell me they are praying for me, and because I know their character I believe them. I've seen hurting people surrounded by a loving church family in prayer. I've seen the church respond with lavish outpouring to those who are in need. I've seen lots of people quietly do their work in the community and in the church, with little fanfare, little applause, and little talk of changing the world, and all the while make a huge difference. I've seen young kids and empty nesters give their lives to help the helpless in Mississippi, or work alongside the poor in Africa, or bring the gospel to college students in Turkey.

I've seen all these things, and a hundred other examples like them, in the un-famous churches I've been a part of. It's easy for the church to be blind to her failings. But it's also easy and borderline slanderous to constantly berate the church for all her failures as if she cared for no one, helped no one, and made no difference for anyone anywhere.

FOR THE LONG HAUL

What we need are fewer revolutionaries and a few more plodding visionaries. That's my dream for the church—God's redeemed people holding tenaciously to a vision of godly obedience and God's glory, and pursuing that godliness and glory with relentless, often unnoticed, plodding consistency.

In doing research for this book, I read three books that had *revolution* in the main title. And in six others I read about our need "for a new revolution, one of love and kindness"[29] and how we need to be more like the first Christians who "revolutionized a predominantly religious world with the eternal spiritual message of God's unconditional love and peace."[30] One book introduced me to Jesus with the words: "Behold your Lord, the Revolutionary!"[31] The church is certainly called to be salt and light—a beacon of truth and a purifying agent in the world, but I see nowhere in Scripture we are charged with being revolutionary-change architects of a new world order.

Now to be fair, there's nothing wrong with wanting a revolution of love or revolution of hope. I could even imagine a good case being made for a revolution of biblical literacy or the like. The problem is that all the talk of revolution suggests that what we need are more Christians ready to check out and overthrow, when by my estimation we need more Christians ready to check in and follow through. As Americans, we are so used to getting what we want, when we want it, and how we want it that when the church is not the way we want it to be we think either (1) "I'm being abused," or (2) "I'm out of here."

My generation in particular is prone to radicalism without follow-through. We have dreams of changing the world, and the world should take notice accordingly. But we've not proved faithful in much of anything yet. We haven't held a steady job or raised godly kids or done our time in VBS or, in some cases, even moved off the parental dole. We want global change and expect the next *Band Aid* or Habit for Humanity chapter to just about wrap things up.

What the church and the world needs from us, we imagine, is to be another Bono—Christian, but more spiritual than religious and more into social justice than the church. As great as it is that Bono is using his fame for some noble purpose, I just don't believe that the happy future of the church, or the world for that matter, rests on our ability to raise up a million more Bonos. With all due respect, what's harder: to be an idolized rock star who travels around the world touting good causes and chiding governments for their lack of foreign aid, or to be a line worker at GM with four kids and a mortgage, who tithes to his church, sings in the praise team every week, serves on the school board, and supports a Christian relief agency and a few missionaries from his disposable income? Even if one is not harder than the other, certainly one is more common. And sadly, that is the one that is more despised.[32]

Until we are content with being one of the million nameless, faceless church members and not the next globe-trotting rock star, we aren't ready to be a part of the church. In the grand scheme of things, most of us are going to be more of an Ampliatus (Rom. 16:8) or Phlegon (16:14) than an apostle Paul. And maybe that's why so many Christians are getting tired of the church. We haven't learned how to be part of the crowd. We haven't learned to live with ordinariness. According to Sweet, Jesus was never bored and boredom is "the ultimate spiritual taboo for a disciple of Jesus."[33] "Spiritual boredom is an oxymoron," writes one church-leaver, "it should be an impossible contradiction. What is from the Spirit is never boring, because it represents the breath of God in our lives."[34] With the bar set this high, it's no wonder we hear young Christians saying things like: "All I wanted was to love Jesus and to get on with life, not go to boring meetings. . . . There was no way any of us was waking up on a Sunday morning, and there was no way that she or her boyfriend would connect with bad 1990s worship music, half hour preaching, and NIV Bibles."[35] We haven't learned the spiritual discipline of being bored for Jesus.

OUR BOREDOM MAY HAVE LESS TO DO WITH THE CHURCH AND ITS DOCTRINES AND MORE TO DO WITH A GROWING COLDNESS TOWARD THE LOVE OF GOD.

Our jobs are often mundane. Our devotional times often seem like a waste. Church services are often forgettable. That's life. We drive to the same places, go through the same routines with our coworkers, buy the same groceries at the store, and mow the same yard every spring and summer. Church is often the same too—same doctrines, same basic order of worship, same preacher, same people. But in all the smallness and sameness, God works—like the smallest seed in the garden growing to unbelievable heights, like beloved Tychicus, that faithful minister, delivering the mail and apostolic greetings (Eph. 6:21). Life is usually pretty ordinary, just like following Jesus most days. Daily discipleship is not a new revolution each morning or an agent of global transformation every evening; it's a long obedience in the same direction.

Of course, we never want to lose our sense of wonder at the gospel. Which, come to think of it, may be why the same old hymns and some old liturgies and same old sermons start sounding stale. It's possible the church needs to change. Certainly in some areas it does. But it's also possible we've changed—and not for the better. It's possible we no longer find joy in so great a salvation. It's possible our boredom and restlessness has less to do with the church and its doctrines and more to do with a growing coldness toward the love of God displayed in the sacrifice of His Son for our sins.

We cannot afford to be fuzzy about the gospel or speak of it with ambiguous euphemisms. The gospel cannot be reduced to: "stay in touch with God and follow your instructions as they are provided." It is not a message about being "available" and staying "firm and focused."[36] Nor is it merely the story of some life-changing experience or the call to community transformation. The gospel is not even the example we give in living out our faith. And it is certainly not an invitation into a Jesus way of life.

In summary, the gospel is not about what we need to do for God. It's a message about what God has done for us. It's the declaration of God's plan of redemption unfolding in history with the death and resurrection of Jesus Christ for the forgiveness of our sins (1 Cor. 15:1–8).

By contrast, the marching orders of the church today are often nothing more than dressed up moralism. We have a gospel of activism, with no rest for the weary, only a summons to do more for the world. This kind of gospel, though it's presented as the glowing alternative to all that suppos-edly plagues the church today, will quickly cause a church to collapse under the weight of its own idealistic demands. We need to recover the doctrine of original sin if for no other reason than so we can once again discover God's glorious grace.

YOU MAY KISS THE BRIDE

The church is not an incidental part of God's plan. Jesus didn't invite people to join an antireligion, antidoctrine, anti-institutional bandwagon of love, harmony, and reintegration. To be sure, He showed people how to live. But He also called them to repent, called them to faith, called them out of the world, and called them into the church.

"Love bears all things, believes all things, hopes all things, endures all things" (1 Cor. 13:7). If we truly love the church we will bear with her in her failings, endure her struggles, believe her to be the beloved bride of Christ, and hope for her final glorification. I still believe the church is the hope of the world—not because she gets it all right, but because she is a body with Christ for her Head.

Don't give up on the church. The New Testament knows nothing of churchless Christianity. The invisible church is for invisible Christians. The visible church is for you and me.[37]

So I guess this is my final advice: Find a good local church, get involved, become a member, stay there for the long haul. Put away thoughts of revolu-tion for a while and join the plodding visionaries. Go to church this Sunday and worship there in spirit and truth, be patient with your leaders, rejoice when the gospel is faithfully proclaimed, bear with those who hurt you, and give people the benefit of the doubt. While you are there, sing like you mean it, say hi to the teenager no one notices, welcome the blue hairs and the nose-ringed, volunteer for the nursery once in a while. And yes, bring your fried chicken to the potluck like everyone else, invite a friend to church, take the new couple out for coffee, give to the Christmas offering, be thankful someone vacuumed the carpet, enjoy the Sundays that click for you, pray extra hard on the Sundays that don't, and do not despise "the day of small things" (Zechariah 4:10).

NOTES

1. Thanks to John Koessler, professor of pastoral studies at Moody Bible Institute, who jump-started our thinking by sharing some of his notes with the folks at Moody Publishers and with us on the "Crisis of Ecclesiology."
2. A welcome exception is the new book by Mark Driscoll and Gary Breshears, *Vintage Church* (Wheaton, Ill.: Crossway, 2009).
3. Brian McLaren, *Everything Must Change* (Nashville: Thomas Nelson, 2007), 103.
4. Steve Chalke and Allan Mann, *The Lost Message of Jesus* (Grand Rapids: Zondervan, 2003), 67.
5. David Tomlinson, *The Post-Evangelical* (Grand Rapids: Zondervan, 2003), 126.
6. Doug Pagitt, *A Christianity Worthy Believing: Hope-Filled, Open-Armed, Alive-and-Well-Faith For the Left Out, Left Behind, and Let Down In Us All* (San Francisco: Jossey-Bass, 2008), 127. Pagitt rejects the doctrine of original sin because otherwise it really is appropriate to make fun of children and tell them they "suck royal" (119), and because he can't stand by as people try to tell his kids that they are evil to the core (130). Instead of original sin, Pagitt believes that the light of God is never completely extinguished from our souls and we are still fearfully and wonderfully made in the image of God. He figures that if original sin is true we are justified in hating people and mocking them and have no reason to see anything decent in humanity. But this is a distorted caricature of original sin. Even Calvin taught that we are still imbued with the "seed of divinity" and that the image of God in us has been marred but not completely destroyed. And obviously we are to treat people kindly and children are precious. None of these scriptural truths negates the other scriptural truths that teach the inherent sinfulness of man.
7. The quotation from Jacobs and the two from Tertullian and Cyprian come from Alan Jacobs, *Original Sin: A Cultural History* (New York: HarperOne, 2008), 32. Jacobs is professor of English at Wheaton College.

8. Jaeson Ma, *The Blueprint: A Revolutionary Plan to Plant Missional Communities on Campus* (Ventura, Calif.: Regal, 2007), 163.

9. Jim Palmer, *Wide Open Spaces* (Nashville: Thomas Nelson, 2007), 36.

10. Andy Morgan, "The Paradox of a Divided Church Called to Be Reconcilers to the World" in Spencer Burke, *Out of the Ooze* (Colorado Springs: NavPress, 2007), 74–75.

11. These descriptions come from Brian Sanders, *Life After Church* (Downers Grove, Ill.: InterVarsity, 2007), 42.

12. See Rodney Stark, *The Rise of Christianity* (San Francisco: HarperCollins, 1997).

13. See Richard Fletcher, *The Barbarian Conversion: From Paganism to Christianity* (Berkeley: Univ. of California Press, 1997).

14. George Barna, to his credit, has a subsection in *Revolution* (Carol Stream, Ill.: Tyndale, 2005), entitled, "This is not Utopia." But yet he concludes the section by saying that the revolution is of "phenomenal significance" and marks a "historic quest for more of God in America" (page 110). It may not be a utopia, but Barna is convinced that revolutionaries will change everything. The church will never be the same. And the world will alter for all time.

15. See Jacobs, *Original Sin*, 209.

16. Theological liberals don't like the doctrine of original sin because it throws a monkey wrench into their plans for societal transformation. If making the world fair and peaceable is the main goal of church, then people everywhere must have the ability in and of themselves to do justice, love mercy, and walk humbly (with God as they understand Him). This approach underlies Brian McLaren's book *Everything Must Change*. See pages 67, 216, 265, 292–93.

17. Sanders, *Life After Church*, 100.

18. Palmer, *Wide Open Spaces*, 197.

19. Sanders, *Life After Church*, 108–109.

20. George Barna, *The Frog in the Kettle* (Ventura, Calif.: Regal, 1990), 111.

21. Ibid., 23.

22. Ibid., 117.

23. Ibid., 119, 146.

24. Ibid., 153.

25. Ibid., 226–230.

26. Ibid., 130.

27. Ibid., 26–27.

28. Sarah Cunningam, a church-leaver herself, at least recognizes this danger in *Dear Church* (Grand Rapids: Zondervan, 2006), 117, 119.

29. William P. Young, *The Shack* (Los Angeles: Windblown Media, 2007), 248.

30. Palmer, *Wide Open Spaces*, 187.

31. Frank Viola and George Barna, *Pagan Christianity* (Carol Stream, ll.: Tyndale, 2008), 246.

32. Leonard Sweet asks rhetorically, "Who has had the greater impact for God and the gospel in the twenty-first century? Any denomination with a million-plus members, or one musician

named Bono?" Leonard Sweet, *The Gospel According to Starbucks* (Colorado Springs: Waterbrook, 2007), 11.

33. Ibid., 8.

34. Sanders, *Life After Church*, 14.

35. Anna Dodridge, quoted in Eddie Gibbs and Ryan K. Bolger, *Emerging Churches* (Grand Rapids: Baker, 2005), 263.

36. Barna, *Revolution*, 95.

37. For more information *about* the local church and *for the benefit of* the local church, there is no better resource out there than 9Marks. Go to their website, www.9marks.org.

ACKNOWLEDGMENTS

It's been a pleasure once again to write a book with Ted. In a day when everyone refers to everyone else as "my good friend so-and-so," Ted actually is my very good friend. My wife and I are fortunate to be in a small group with Ted and Kristin, and when our sons aren't bloodying each other and destroying the basement drywall, I'm thankful that our kids can be friends too. If our two books together accomplished nothing besides cementing our friendship, that would be well worth it.

I'm grateful to work with the Wolgemuth gang and all the good people at Moody. Sometimes I wonder why they keep helping me publish books. But so far they haven't stopped. Go figure.

My parents made me go to church every Sunday, morning and evening, plus Sunday school, and Wednesday evening, and almost anything else that came along. What a lot of hours they made me spend in church, and what a blessing. They never seemed to mind going to church, so I didn't much either.

I have yet to be a part of a perfect church (a trend that will certainly continue with me as pastor of my church). But I have been immensely helped by all the churches I've attended. I was baptized in First Reformed Church in South Holland, Illinois. I made my profession of faith and grew up under the gospel at Hager Park Reformed Church in Jenison, Michigan. I loved the teaching and preaching at my college church, Immanuel Baptist Church in Holland, Michigan. While studying in seminary, I met a host of godly, capable, fun, intelligent, committed Christians who welcomed me in with open arms at First Presbyterian Church in Ipswich, Massachusetts. I got my feet wet and received loving support as an associate pastor at First Reformed Church in Orange City, Iowa. And now I have the immense privilege to serve the people at University Reformed Church in East Lansing, Michigan. Hardly a Sunday goes by when I don't say to my wife, "We have a really great church with a lot of good people."

One of the blessings of being in pastoral ministry is getting to connect with other pastors. Since writing *Why We're Not Emergent* I've been privileged to meet a number of like-minded pastors, a few well known, but most quietly doing their ministries with little recognition. I have benefited from interactions with all of them. I'm especially thankful for the pastors I meet with on a regular basis: Dale Van Dyke from Grand Rapids, and in a different group, Doug Phillips and Jason Helopolous from the Lansing area. The church in North America looks bleak at times, but there are a lot of good pastors and churches still out there—more than we often realize.

As always, my wife, Trisha, has been my constant support. How she takes care of the kids and me, I don't know. But she does it well, and almost always with a smile. Honey, since the kids haven't thought to do so yet, let me rise up and call you "blessed." Many women have done excellently, but as far as I'm concerned, you keep surpassing all the other moms out there (Proverbs 31:28–29).

Kevin DeYoung

✻ ✻ ✻

It's a weird stage, in the life cycle of a book, to realize that you're ready to write the acknowledgments. When I got my first book deal, I think I wrote the acknowledgments before I penned the first chapter of the book, because I was so eager to thank my parents, my friends, my grade-school teacher who believed in me, etc. That was stupid and a little arrogant, and I'm sure if I went back and read those acknowledgments now, I would be appalled at their sappiness. And authors do this—that is, they go back and read their acknowledgments, even wanting that oft-forgotten portion of the book to sound sweet.

That said, I knew it was time to pen the acknowledgments after I had dinner with Dave, a friend of mine. Dave is dogmatic. Dave has no problem standing up for what he believes in, and arguing about doctrine. He actually enjoys this, so I go to Dave when I need a pep talk, which I needed when I was knee-deep in my Internet brouhaha over *Purple State of Mind* (see chapter 4). So thanks, Dave, for your friendship, and for encouraging your less-bold friend to contend earnestly for the faith.

Aside: You may be reading this and thinking, "Why don't I get an individual shout-out in the acknowledgments, like Dave here?" Fear not—I probably thanked you by name in the *Facing Tyson* acknowledgments, because I think I thanked everyone I had ever met in that one.

I want to thank my great friends at University Reformed Church in East

Lansing, a place I'm proud to call my church home. (P.S.: Don't be mad over chapter 2.) Thanks to Kevin, who is a very gifted writer, a talented preacher, and an even greater friend. You, Trisha, and the kids are a blessing to us.

Thanks to Chuck Colson and Dawn Clark for the great interviews, and to John Marks and Craig Detweiler for being willing to dialogue with someone like me. Thanks to Albert Mohler and Alistair Begg for preaching exposi-tional preaching.

Thanks too, to our good friends at Moody Publishing, Dave DeWit and Tracey Shannon, who always make us feel at home in Chicago (tell the babushkas at Jenkins Hall we said hello) and always shepherd us through these books with love and wisdom. And to my agent, Andrew Wolgemuth, who is my ambassador of kwan, a great friend, and is also really good at what he does.

Thanks, again, to my parents, for dragging me to church all those years. At some point along the way I really started liking it, and, truth be told, I always kind of liked it, even when I was drawing on my bulletin. More than that, I liked being with you, and sitting beside you in the pew every Sunday. You guys are, literally, a God-send, and I thank Him for you both, every day.

And finally, to Kristin. I want the world (or at least the several thousand people who buy this book) to know how amazing you are. Everything I do I do in a usually ill-fated attempt to impress you, and despite my bumbling, you love me anyway. You're kind, forgiving, funny, and beautiful. You and Tristan are my favorite people in the whole, wide world. You'll be a little embarrassed by that but it looks good in print. Yeah, it really does.

Ted Kluck

Why We're Not Emergent

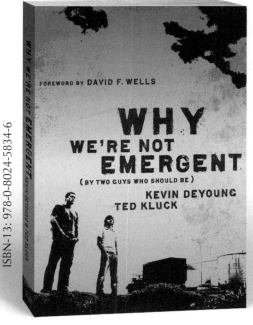

FOREWORD BY DAVID F. WELLS

WHY WE'RE NOT EMERGENT

(BY TWO GUYS WHO SHOULD BE)

KEVIN DEYOUNG
TED KLUCK

ISBN-13: 978-0-8024-5834-6

2009
Christianity Today
Book Award
Winner!

"You can be young, passionate about Jesus Christ, surrounded by diversity, engaged in a postmodern world, reared in evangelicalism and not be an emergent Christian. In fact, I want to argue that it would be better if you weren't."

The emergent church is a strong voice in today's Christian community. And they're talking about good things: caring for the poor, peace for all men, loving Jesus. They're doing church a new way, not content to fit the mold. Again, all good. But there's more to the movement than that. Much more.

Kevin DeYoung and Ted Kluck are two guys who, demographically, should be all over this movement. But they're not. And *Why We're Not Emergent* gives you the solid reasons why. From both a theological and an on-the-street perspective, Kevin and Ted diagnose the emerging church. They pull apart interviews, articles, books, and blogs, helping you see for yourself what it's all about.

1-800-678-8812 • MOODYPUBLISHERS.COM

JUST DO SOMETHING

ISBN-13: 978-0-8024-5838-4

Hyper-spiritual approaches to finding God's will just don't work. It's time to try something new: give up. Pastor and author Kevin DeYoung counsels Christians to settle down, make choices, and do the hard work of seeing those choices through. Too often, he writes, God's people jump from church to church, workplace to workplace, relational circle to relational circle, worrying that they haven't found God's perfect will for their lives. But God doesn't need to tell us what to do at each fork in the road. He's already revealed His plan for our lives: to love Him with our whole hearts, to obey His Word, and after that, to do what we like. No need for hocus-pocus. No reason to be directionally challenged. Just do something.

THE REASON FOR SPORTS

ISBN-13: 978-0-8024-5836-0

There are books on how to worship God with our marriages, our money, and our sex lives. Books on how to "think biblically" about movies, television and the arts. Books on how to vote Christianly and how not to vote Christianly. But there is little thoughtful, Christ-centered writing on the subject that drives most of men's banter with each other and consumes the bulk of their free time. Sports. Written in the vein of Rick Reilly (*Sports Illustrated*), Chuck Klosterman (*Spin, Esquire*), and David Foster Wallace (*A Supposedly Fun Thing I'll Never Do Again*), *The Reason for Sports* will both entertain and shed light on some of today's most pertinent sports issues: race, drugs, hero worship, and more - all through a biblical lens.

1-800-678-8812 • MOODYPUBLISHERS.COM